Data Processing
A First Course

To Roslyn and Amanda

Data Processing
A First Course

David Harrison

Pitman

PITMAN PUBLISHING LIMITED
128 Long Acre, London WC2E 9AN

Associated Companies
Pitman Publishing Pty Ltd, Melbourne
Pitman Publishing New Zealand Ltd, Wellington

© D Harrison 1983

First published in Great Britain 1983
Reprinted 1983

Printed in Great Britain at The Pitman Press, Bath

ISBN 0 273 01887 6

Contents

Acknowledgments

I would like to thank Brenda Paisley and Judith Parker for all the work they have done on the Fashion 85 project.

The author and publishers would also like to thank the following for permission to reproduce material:

IBM UK Limited
NCR Limited
Honeywell Information Systems Limited
British Rail Eastern Region
Banking Information Service

Introduction

Data processing as an activity has been around since the cave dwellers became farmers. Ug and Og, the prehistoric equivalent of 'the Archers', would let their animals out into the fields during the day and then round them up again at night. As a check to make sure that animals were not lost they invented the tally stick. Ug would cut a notch in a stick every time an animal passed him going into the fields and he would tick off the notches against the animals passing him on the way home. Even though he could not count he had a record of the number of animals he was supposed to have and could easily check whether any had been lost or stolen.

The need for data and data processing grew as populations expanded and trade increased. William the Conqueror carried out massive data processing projects. He commissioned the *Domesday Book*, recording ownership, use and value of all of the land in England. The amount of data processing being carried out gradually increased until the mid-twentieth century.

The advent of computers in the 1940s, and more particularly the adoption of the computer for business purposes in the 1950s, has led to a tremendous increase in the amount of data being processed. This is sometimes called the 'information explosion'—a somewhat misleading term since this growth is still going on. The fact that this has come about because of the development of the computer has meant that computing and data processing have come to mean the same thing, yet, as can be seen from the example set by Ug and Og, data can easily be processed without a system of numbers, let alone a sophisticated computer system.

It is the purpose of this book to discuss data processing in its widest sense, not just the computerised version, which should really be given its proper term—**electronic data processing** (EDP).

1 Data and information

The term 'data' refers to the facts and figures relating to events that take place. A dictionary defines **data** as 'things known' and **information** as 'items of knowledge'. The distinction is not very clear so we must look elsewhere to find the difference between data and information.

Data may relate to figures, so if we examine some numbers it may help to show the difference between the two terms.

    18   36   180

These numbers convey very little in terms of meaning. Adding further details will add to the amount of information they give.

    18 years   36 Pit Road   £180

This gives us more information but it is still not absolutely clear what the data refers to.

James Smith is 18 years old, lives at 36 Pit Road and has £180 in his bank account.

In this form we have a lot of information in a form which is useful to us, but it is long winded. We have processed some *data* to provide *information*.

The purpose of data processing is to collect and record facts and figures relating to events and present them as meaningful information in a concise form.

Almost everything we do involves some form of data processing. We are born and the fact is recorded in several places. When we attend school note is taken of our attendance. If we are ill, the facts relating to the illness are recorded by the doctor. As we get older the amount of data recorded about us increases; details of bank accounts, wages earned and tax paid. To drive a car we must have road tax and insurance as well as a driving licence. All of these things require facts and figures to be collected and recorded.

Exercise 1

1 Make a list of all of the organisations which recorded the fact that you were born, eg if you were born in a hospital a record of the fact will be kept in the hospital files.
2 Assume that you have bought a second-hand car from a friend. It is not taxed or insured but it has an MOT certificate. As you have never driven before, your

father has offered to give you driving lessons. Find out how many forms you will have to fill in before you can put the car on the road.

In everyday life we are constantly bombarded with raw data by our senses. We process this data by trying to put it into context. If we manage to put the data into a recognisable context we can then use the information provided to help us to make decisions; otherwise we disregard the data.

For example, we may receive a signal from our eyes saying 'red dress'. Until we can put this into context it is meaningless. A girl going to a dance might notice that her best friend is wearing a red dress and this information could then be used to help her to decide what she should wear herself. A boutique manager may notice that a large number of girls in the street are wearing red dresses. This data could then result in the conclusion that red is a fashionable colour, which in turn would influence his decision when he places his next order with his supplier.

In some circumstances the same piece of data takes on different meanings depending on how and where the information is used. The data item £5000 gives little information on its own. Put into context, 'I owe £5000' obviously has a very different meaning from 'I have just won £5000'.

Quantitative and qualitative data

Data can be divided into two types. **Qualitative data** can be said to describe an item or to relate to its quality. **Quantitative data** relates to the size or amount of data. These two types of data can be either **alphanumeric** (or alphameric) or **numeric**. The first of these terms comes from a combination of the words 'alphabetic' and 'numeric' and means data items consisting of letters, numbers and other symbols. Numeric data consists of numbers. Quantitative data may have some units, eg centimetres, hours, etc, connected with it, and this type of data can be used to perform meaningful arithmetic.

Consider the number D845360. This contains letters and figures, and therefore it is alphanumeric. It could be used as a code number or account number. The digits 845360 by themselves could represent a telephone number. If so, then any arithmetic carried out on this number would be meaningless. Even though it consists entirely of numbers this item is alphanumeric; the number can only be treated as a set of figures (eight–four–five–three–six–zero) rather than as a single number. However, if the number represented the quantity of items in stock then this would be a numeric data item and arithmetic carried out on this value would have some meaning. A data item like £153 563 printed on a bill consists of symbols and figures. The whole item is considered to be an alphanumeric item, but the £ sign really represents the units used. This means that the numbers can be represented as a quantitative item and meaningful arithmetic can be carried out.

Exercise 2

1 Consider the following extract from a letter of application for a job at a company called Fashion 85.

> Dear Sir,
> With reference to the vacancy you advertised in the *Daily News* on <u>Friday 29 September</u> for an office junior, I would like to be considered for this position.
> I am <u>17 years old</u> and attended the West Park Comprehensive School, Westpool from the age of <u>11 years</u>. During my last 2 years at school I chose to follow a general course with a clerical bias, at the end of which I was entered for 'O' level and CSE examinations. I was involved in a broad range of activities and studies that included sports, personal relationships, environmental and social problems, and a variety of leisure pursuits. Although I was not a very active member, I belonged to the School Swimming Club and worked for the Schools Community Aid Committee. My examination results were: <u>'O' level English Language (B)</u> and Art (B), and CSE Geography <u>(Grade 3)</u>, Typing <u>20wpm (Grade 2)</u> and Social Studies (Grade 4). I was re-entered for a <u>Typing 25wpm</u> examination in the late summer and await the result. Since leaving school I have been attending the College of Further Education where I am now working for a BEC General award.

a After reading the extract, state which of the underlined data items is *qualitative* and which is *quantitative*.
b If the date of the advertisement had been written as 29.10.8–, would it be quantitative or qualitative?
c Say whether the following are quantitative or qualitative:

- the post code CV3 5DW
- the telephone number 021 563 5687
- the bank account number 2345676
- the bank balance £34.78
- the number of people in the class 17
- the height of a person 1.6 m.

Assignment 1

1 You are U R Keen, the office junior at Fashion 85. You are attending a day release course at Westpool College of Further Education studying, among other things, data processing. You are involved in the students' union of the college, which organises activities such as dances, discos and sports. As a result of the data processing course you have become aware of several things about data, and you realise that at college, at work and in your everyday life you are in contact with raw data that is only meaningful if looked at in context. For example, each of the following is taken from Fashion 85 data, but it is meaningless without a label.

- VEF 153B
- 40 degrees
- Frank
- 0937 75453
- Green
- 36 24 36
- 1300L
- 050680

Attach a label to each of the above to make them meaningful.

2   As part of your involvement in the college student union you are required to organise activities like dances, discos and sporting events for students. What *type* of information would you expect new members to provide so that you could do this? Give examples.

3   Your colleague, Justine Thyme, is 18 years old. She was born on 15-3-62 at the Westpool General Hospital. Most people think she is an attractive girl. She is 5 feet tall with red hair, brown eyes and a 34–23–34 figure. By careful dieting she keeps her weight to 7 stone. At present she lives with her parents at 23 Stockfield Road, Westpool, and her telephone number is Westpool 375842. When she was younger she used to go ice skating but her main interest now is disco dancing. Her favourite food is yoghurt and her favourite colour is blue. She thinks her lucky number is 8.

a Write down the headings *Quantitative* and *Qualitative*. Under the appropriate headings list the items of data relating to Justine from the passage.

b Write down the items from the above passage which you think would be: useful to boys; useful to girls; of little practical use to anybody.

4   Quantitative data usually has some units associated with it. Copy out the following table and fill in as many units as you can find for each entry.

Data item	Units
Length of item Area of item Temperature Speed Length of time Power	

5   In what way is the table of contents of a book different from the index?

2 Information in organisations

Organisations consist of interrelated systems and subsystems. A system consists of a set of functions and procedures. If we consider a library, for example, we can describe the way it functions as follows:

In order to carry out these functions a great deal of information is required. Let us consider each subsystem.

1

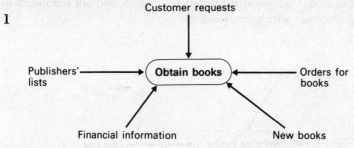

In order to *obtain books* data must be received in the form of lists of titles available, requests from customers for particular books and financial information (how much money is available). This data is organised and the information which results is used to decide which books should be purchased. The orders can then be sent out and shortly afterwards the new books should arrive.

2

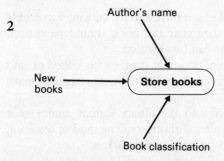

To *store* the books information is required to enable the book to be placed on the shelf in the correct place. The name of the book and the author's name are required to enable the book to be entered on the catalogue.

3

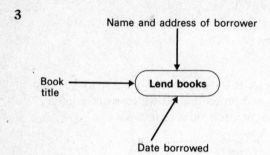

Before books can be lent by a library data must be collected relating to the title of the book, the name and address of the borrower and the date on which the book was borrowed. This data is obtained from the book and the borrower's ticket and the information can be used to send out reminders to customers with books which are overdue.

4

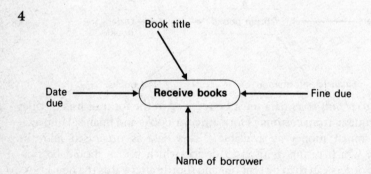

When books are checked in the ticket is returned to the customer to enable him to borrow more books. The date that the book should have been returned can be checked and any fine can be collected.

Each section of the library system requires data to be collected and processed to form information which can be used by the librarians to make decisions.

All of the sections are interrelated and the library system cannot exist without all of these subsystems. A library without some method of receiving books, for example, will quickly end up with empty shelves.

Exercise 3

1 Visit a library and write some notes on:

    a Dewey decimal system
    b library catalogue
    c method of deciding which new books are to be obtained.

2 Make a list of the items of data recorded on a library ticket.

Commercial systems can be shown as illustrated in the diagrams below. In these examples the *sales system* is a subsystem of the *production system* since the goods have to be sold once they have been produced. Materials have to be paid for and goods must be stored.

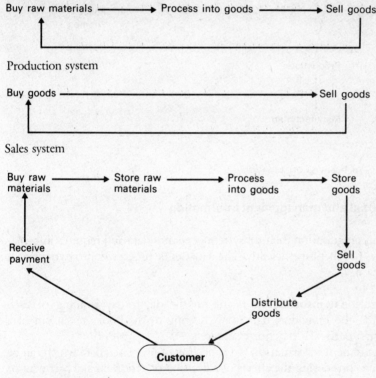

Buy raw materials ⟶ Process into goods ⟶ Sell goods

Production system

Buy goods ⟶ Sell goods

Sales system

Buy raw materials ⟶ Store raw materials ⟶ Process into goods ⟶ Store goods

Receive payment

Sell goods

Distribute goods

Customer

Manufacturing system

Types of organisation

Business organisations can be divided into a variety of groups (see below). The function of these various organisations is to supply goods and services. Industry, commerce and business services exist to make a profit and this enables the social services to be financed from taxation.

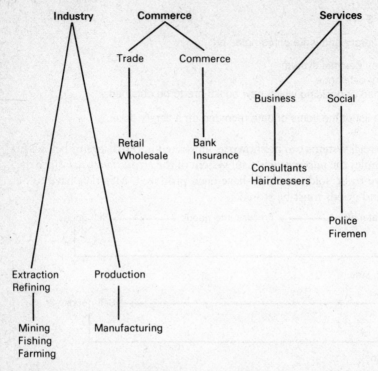

The variety of business organisations

Operational and management information

Within an organisation each subsystem generates data and requires information if it is to function efficiently. The data can be processed into two types of information.

1 **Operational information** relates to the day-to-day running of each subsystem—the individual data items relating to the books taken out of a library on a particular day, for example.
2 **Management information** is a collection of processed data which can be used when considering the effects of a decision or action on a department or section of an organisation—the amount of money a library has to spend on books, for example.

Fashion 85 Wages Department processes large quantities of data relating to the hours worked by its employees. Payslips are produced and wage packets are made up. At the same time reports are produced to show the heads of department how much is being spent on wages. This information can be used to help when negotiating pay rises, and so is considered to be *management information*. The payslip issued to an employee is *operational information*.

If management information is to be useful it must have certain qualities.

1 It must be **relevant**. All of the information supplied must be important to the person receiving it. If he is given information which is not important then he wastes his time reading it.

2 It must be **complete**. No information should be missed out.

3 It must be **timely**. It is no good giving a person information this week when the decisions based on that information had to be made last week.

4 It must be **accurate**. Decisions based on poor information cannot be good ones.

5 It must be **well presented**. Managers are busy people who will take in more information if it is presented in an attractive way. They will have no time to sort through badly presented reports to find the required information.

6 It should be **cost effective**. It is expensive to collect and process data. People employed in data processing have to be paid and materials have to be paid for. This means that only essential data processing should be carried out.

Exercise 4

1 Copy the following table:

Industry		Commerce		Services	
Refining	Production	Trade	Commerce	Business	Social

Fill in the names of the following companies in the appropriate columns:

a British Steel Corporation
b BL Motors Ltd
c Rolls Royce Aerospace
d Phoenix Insurance Co Ltd

e St Johns Ambulance Brigade
f The Samaritans
g Flowers Anonymous (Florists) Limited
h RHM Foods Limited

(cont)

i West Hill Farm
j British Road Services
k Consumer Advice Centre
l Trimfit Sauna Limited
m Barclays Bank Limited

n Hair Eight Salon
o Secretarial Services Agency
p British Nuclear Fuels Ltd
q British Midland Airways

2 Annette Profitt was fed up. As a bookkeeper with Fashion 85 it had been one of
those weeks. She was in the middle of recording expense claims for the week
but her mind was on the fact that she considered she was overworked and
underpaid. This week she had worked two hours overtime and next week
she would have to do more. The number of petty cash vouchers alone had
been increasing every week for months now; she had already recorded ten
more this week than last and several claims still had not come in. Picking up the
next voucher she made a mental note that Luke Sharpe must have been on
another trip since that was the fifth claim he had made that month and as she
added on the value it occurred to her that the total petty cash expenditure for
that month must be at least 14 per cent higher than the previous month. Still,
that was inflation for you. She consoled herself with the fact that she would be
on holiday in two weeks' time, soaking up the sun in Corfu.

Read through the passage above. Write down two headings: *Operational
Information* and *Management Information*. Under the appropriate headings write
down as many pieces of information about Fashion 85 as possible from the
passage.

Fashion 85

Our company has developed considerably since it was founded in 1912. It
has adapted to changing times by using mass production methods and
modern technology, but we are still primarily concerned with producing
garments of a high quality. In order to retain our links with the past the
premises occupied by our founder in 1912 are now used as Head Office. An
extension to the building became a new factory. As the demand for our goods
grew nationally other factories were established in places where good
communications facilities were available. We now have factories in Mother-
well, Westpool, Sale, Nottingham, Milton Keynes and Cardiff. We have
recently negotiated the lease of a site at Bromley for our factory of the 1990s.

We have a flexible organisation. We not only initiate production in
response to market information and thereby lead in the fashion world, but
also undertake contracts for large retail stores. Although some of the
administration is carried out in each factory, the greater part is centred on the
Head Office in Westpool. Our administrative structure consists of seven
departments including the production unit attached to Head Office.

Morris Makepiece is the head of the Production Department and he is
responsible for the overall supervision of the factory and the planning of new
methods of production. He works closely with other heads of departments,

eg with the Personnel Officer concerning safety and working conditions, with the Purchases Department for the supply of raw materials and with the Accounts Department by keeping records of manufacturing costs. He is ably assisted by Ernest Foreman, the maintenance engineer, who plans and supervises the work of five mechanics and who deputises for Morris Makepiece if necessary. Other staff in the department number 297: 5 cutters, 10 supervisors, 280 machinists and pressers and 2 ticket clerks.

Attached to the Production Department are the loading bays and garage of the Transport Department, the responsibility of Roland Wheeler. He is assisted by Austin Carr and a team of clerks and motor mechanics. The Department is responsible for the overall care of a fleet of vehicles and keeps records of each, including running costs, mileage and maintenance. So that only authorised goods are taken from the premises the Department issues despatch copies of the invoices and keeps a record of goods delivered and goods returned. In the yard are the company's own petrol and diesel pumps, and the clerks who work in the Department keep a simple logbook to record the quantities of fuel supplied to each vehicle. Most of the goods that are transported in our vehicles are for delivery to our customers who have placed orders as a result of the activities of our sales force.

The sales force is controlled by the head of the department, Mark Sellers, whose private secretary is Anita Page. In addition to the overall responsibility for the work of the Sales Department, Mark Sellers directs a sales force made up of five United Kingdom Area Managers each of whom leads and supervises four representatives. Since the United Kingdom became a member of the European Economic Community it has become company policy to sell in Europe. Miles Long and two representatives, one based in Brussels and the other in Rome, are involved in building a sales network throughout Europe.

The representatives are important, not only because they obtain orders, but also because they provide useful feedback of information the company needs to determine future sales policy. The implementation of sales policy is the responsibility of Mark Sellers, who has an assistant, Luke Sharpe, to take charge in his absence. Luke's chief function is the design of Fashion 85 garments. There are two clothes designers to assist him.

Also in this Department is Bonny Barker, the Public Relations Officer, who leads a team of three working on the design of advertising material for Fashion 85 garments. They are involved in the preparation and presentation of a wide range of items from price tickets to mannequin parades.

Once the design of a garment has been approved for production, the items that go into its manufacture must be obtained. The purchase of such items, at the right time and price, in the right quantity and of the right quality, is the responsibility of the Purchases Department under the direction of Jean Byers, the head of the department, and M T Pockett, her assistant. These factors of price, quantity and quality, are also important in the purchase of all the other items the company buys, eg machines, office furniture, buildings, maintenance equipment and even foodstuffs. Because the company buys so many different types of articles the work of the Purchases Department is split into sections. Heather Tweedi and two buyers concentrate on the purchase of raw materials such as fabrics; Georgette Lacy and two buyers deal with trimmings; all maintenance and capital expenditure items are under the control of Ivor Bolt; while Abel Cooke is in charge of items related to catering. Gerda Sample is the person who gives secretarial assistance to all the buyers.

The financial side of all the company's buying is controlled by the Accounts Department, as is stock, costing, the payment of wages and salaries and the recording of transactions. Tilley Spencer is our accountant and financial adviser to the Board of Directors. Her duties include the preparation of the annual accounts, to be presented at the Annual General Meeting, and dealing with the company's tax liability. Her private secretary is Olive Etty.

Originally the Accounts Department was the first within the company to use computer equipment. Over the years this use has increased to the extent that a large proportion of the company depends on the Computing Section for its data processing requirements. In the next few years it is expected that a major reorganisation will take place and that as a result the Data Processing Section will become a large department in its own right.

The work of the Accounts Department is carried out by five Section Heads.

1   Bob Tanner heads the Costing Section and is Tilley Spencer's deputy. His main responsibility is the analysis of production costs with the purpose of increasing the profit of the company.
2   Ed Sorter is in charge of the Data Processing Section. He is responsible for all of the data processing systems within Fashion 85. Generally this is confined to the computerised systems and those areas which may be put on to the computer in the future. He has two assistants, one to look after the programming requirements and the other one to look after the day-to-day running of the system. The section also includes a Data Control Supervisor and four clerks, Data Preparation Supervisor and six operators, six computer operators and a programming team.
3   Andrew Pounds heads the Wages and Salaries Section.
4   Will Stack looks after the Stock Control Section.
5   Annette Profitt heads the Bookkeeping Section.

Most of the accounting data used to be recorded using accounting machines which produced punched tape for feeding into a computer, but in recent years computing equipment has been obtained that has allowed the Accounts Department to operate more efficiently. The handful of specialist staff which had to be taken on to operate the equipment and prepare data for input to the system were necessary in view of the recent expansion that has taken place in the company.

The Personnel Department has direct responsibility to every other department. Its head is Hiram Clarke and Anne Addler is his secretary. While he is chiefly concerned with the recruitment of staff, his three assistants deal with training and education, welfare and industrial relations. In addition to recruitment, Hiram keeps staff records and staff progress reports. These may be needed for promotions, transfers and references. Part of the work of the Training–Education Officer, Julie Trainor, is to assess what training schemes are needed and to make arrangements for various kinds of training to take place.

Amy Love is the Welfare Officer and she is responsible for ensuring that the working conditions comply with the legal requirements. She is also in charge of the canteen, cloakroom, washing, sports and recreational facilities. The Welfare Officer is the person to whom any employee may turn when faced with personal problems.

The specialist care of the kitchen is in the care of Adam Pybaker and Ivor Honeyman with their staff of a cook, two assistant cooks, four kitchen assistants and a waitress.

Discipline, internal disputes, negotiations with unions and safety are dealt with by O B Fair, the Industrial Relations Officer.

In addition to its responsibilities towards the staff in all departments, the Personnel Department is responsible to the management for obtaining the best staff, for using them in the best way and for ensuring that they stay with the company.

Whereas every other department is concerned with some specific aspect of the company's business, the Office is responsible for providing services for them all. The head of the Office, Frank Stamper, is the Company Secretary. His duties include general office administration, the keeping of various books and returns required by law, the organisation of directors' and shareholders' meetings and the implementation of decisions taken at them. He has an Office Manager, Colin Askew, who deals with the day-to-day running of the Office including the ordering and care of stationery and other office supplies. He also organises contract work, eg cleaning. His private secretary, Patience Groom, is also responsible for the typists in the typing pool and the clerks who work in the Office. The other staff in the department are two receptionists, two switchboard operators, a junior, three operators in the print room, a commissionaire, Sean Porter, and a security officer, N E Ware.

Who's who in Fashion 85

Board of Directors
Gen B E C Aymes (ret), DSO (Chairman)

M A K Headway, JP
A Ward, BSc(Econ)
R T Tuck, FRCA
David Cholmondley Smythe
Dame Margot H Manberry
Ken Maddrick, FIS
Tilley Spencer, BSc, ICA (Financial Adviser)
Frank Stamper, BA, FCIS (Company Secretary)
Airey Coates (Managing Director)

The departments

Accounts	Head of Department	Tilley Spencer
	Data Processing Manager	Ed Sorter, MBCS
	Senior Systems Analyst	N Quire, MBCS
	Secretary	Olive Etty
	Costing	Bob Tanner
	Wages/Salaries	Andrew Pounds
	Stock Control	Will Stack
	Data Prep. Supervisor	Vera Dijou
	Operations Manager	Cardew Loader
	Data Control Supervisor	Mags Tapper
	Bookkeeping	Annette Profitt
Production	Head of Department	Morris Makepiece
	Assistant	Ernest Foreman
Purchases	Head of Department	Jean Byers
	Secretary	Gerda Sample
	Assistant	M T Pockett
	Materials	Heather Tweedie
	Trimmings	Georgette Lacy
	Maintenance	Ivor Bolt
	Catering	Abel Cooke
Sales	Head of Department	Mark Sellers
	Secretary	Anita Page
	Assistant (Design)	Luke Sharpe
	Assistant (Publicity)	Bonny Barker
	Export Manager	Miles Long
Personnel	Head of Department	Hiram Clarke
	Training Officer	Julie Trainor
	Welfare Officer	Amy Love
	Industrial Relations Officer	O B Fair
	Secretary	Anne Addler

Transport	Head of Department	Roland Wheeler
	Assistant	Austin Carr
The Office	Head of Department	Frank Stamper
	Office Manager	Colin Askew
	Secretary	Patience Groom
	Receptionists	Polly Esther Cotton
		U Golightly
	Switchboard	Percy Vearance
		Justine Thyme
	Junior	U R Keen
	Commissionaire	Sean Porter
	Security Officer	N E Ware

Fashion 85 can be shown diagrammatically as a series of interlinked systems and subsystems As can be seen the information flow within the company is very complex. Each system relates to every other system inside the company and to systems within the suppliers' companies and the customers' companies. The main part of Fashion 85 is the Production system but within the framework of the company the Office and Personnel Department provide essential services. Take away any one part and the whole company cannot carry on functioning.

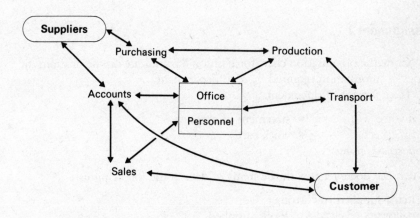

Each department requires a large amount of management information to allow heads of departments to make decisions relating to methods of working, eg operational information is required to keep a check on day-to-day performance. The information may be recorded in many different ways depending on how it is to be used.

Exercise 5

1 Write down the main functions of the Purchasing and Production Departments.
2 When the payroll is made up every week certain items have to be recorded. Find out what these items are.
3 Colin Askew is responsible for ordering and care of stationery supplies. In order to make sure he is never short of important items he will have to keep records of supplies taken from the store. List the items of operational data which he will need to record. Are there any items of management information which he will require to allow him to do this part of his job properly?

The organisation of Fashion 85 is typical of any manufacturing company. It is important to realise that a lot of jobs in the company are concerned with data processing. Management must decide on how many garments should be produced each week, how many people will be needed to make them, and how much it will cost to make them. Related directly to the cost of production is the cost of running each factory and office. Services have to be paid for—gas, electricity and rates do not come free to industry. The type of garments produced will have to be decided on and the cost to the customer. The cost of transport and the type of transport to use is also an important management decision. To make these decisions information relating to the cost of raw materials, the time taken to produce each type of garment and the wages earned in making them has to be collected, along with many other pieces of information about the suppliers, customers and employees.

Assignment 2

1 Copy the organisation chart for Fashion 85. Indicate on the diagram the types of information required by each department.
2 Here is a list of documents:

- invoice
- timesheet
- despatch note
- statement of account
- clock card

Match the documents with the items of data in the following list:

- items supplied to customer
- payments received for goods supplied
- payments required for goods supplied
- details of hours worked by employees
- starting and finishing times for each employee

3 When you start your job as an office junior with Fashion 85 Frank Stamper shows you around the department. Explain what he might say is the main function of his department.

Denham House, Weavers Way
WESTPOOL Cleveland CV3 5DW

Telephone: Westpool (0937) 47632 3 4
Telex: 152773
Telegraphic Address: DENWAY WESTPOOL

FASHION 85 LIMITED

STOCK REQUISITION

Requisition No

Department

Date

Quantity	Description	Usual Supplier	Received By

Signed

Authorised by:

Stock requisition form

(This form may be reproduced if desired.)

4 As office junior you are given a piece of paper on which Patience Groom has jotted a brief note of the office requirements.

2000 manilla plain envelopes
2000 long banker's envelopes (white)
      Bic crystal pens   fine point   2 doz each   blue/black
      Bic crystal pens   medium point   2 doz each   blue/black
   20 Reams A4 typing paper   18 lb
   50 Reams A4 typing paper   21 lb

a Explain what information you would require before you could place the order.
b Use the extract from the Office Supplies catalogue (see Appendix 1) to fill in the stock requisition form on page 17 to be passed to the Accounts Department for approval.
c Copy out the following passage and fill in the blanks with the names of the appropriate forms.

When you have filled in the requisition it is passed to the Accounts Department. If it is approved an .... is sent to Office Supplies Ltd. A credit check is carried out and the order is made up. Fashion 85 receive the goods along with a .... which gives details of the goods. The Accounts Department will be informed of how much is owed as they will get an .... sent to them. Every month Office Supplies send Fashion 85 a .... giving details of the month's transactions.

5 Every few years the Fashion 85 car fleet becomes due for renewal. Roland Wheeler has to recommend new models to replace the present ones. This is an important decision which will result in the company spending a lot of money. Roland is a good manager who usually bases his decisions on sound data. Make a list of the data items on which he would base his report.

3 Media

The material on which data and information is recorded is called the **recording medium** (plural media). Many different materials are available for data recording. The tally sticks mentioned in the introduction were media for recording the number of animals.

The medium used for recording a particular set of data will depend upon how the data will be stored and processed.

Card index

A card index is a method of storing data for quick reference. Each item has its data recorded on a separate card. These cards are called records and they may be typed or handwritten. All of the cards relating to the same type of item are called a card index file. The cards may then be stored vertically in a box or drawer which is only slightly wider than the cards themselves (see below).

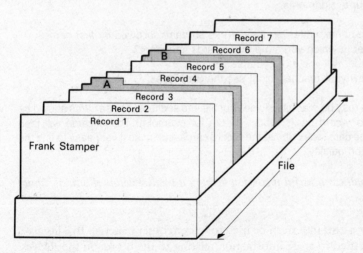

A card index

```
┌─────────────────────────────────────────────────────────────────┐
│  Surname ················          First name(s) ·················· │
│                                    ································· │
│  Class/Course no  ······································            │
│  Address ······································                     │
│  ····································································· │
│  ···································································   │
│  Grades obtained   ┌────┬────┬────┬────┬────┬────┬────┬────┐      │
│  Assignment no     │ 1  │ 2  │ 3  │ 4  │ 5  │ 6  │ 7  │ 8  │      │
│                    └────┴────┴────┴────┴────┴────┴────┴────┘      │
└─────────────────────────────────────────────────────────────────┘
```

Index card

Exercise 6

Each member of your group should obtain a piece of thin cardboard (approximately 15 cm by 10 cm will be sufficient).

This card will be used for your record in a class card index system which will be useful to your tutor.

Make a copy of the index card illustrated (write or type the headings) and fill in as many details as possible.

Collect together all of the cards for your class or group and store them in a box where they can be kept vertically. Keep these cards up to date by filling in the grades for your assignments.

1 Why is the name written on the card as *surname* followed by *first name*?
2 Is the order in which you store these cards important?
3 In what order will you store your cards.
4 Explain how your teacher might use the card index.

Index cards may be made to divide your file into sections. These cards should be taller than the record cards (about 11 cm for example). These cards will then stand out of the card index above the record cards and make it very easy to find the required section quickly.

The card index is a useful method of keeping a small amount of data for quick reference.

Sometimes a card index can be used to refer to other material. In a library a card index is used to store information relating to the books on the shelves. This can be used to find out if a particular book is available.

Assignment 3

Hiram Clarke, the Personnel Manager, has decided that as well as the normal personnel files which he has in his office it would be useful to have a card index system containing records of every member of staff. This decision resulted from a telephone call he received recently. The caller, a young girl, was obviously very upset and was calling to ask if somebody could tell her sister that their mother had been rushed into hospital. All that Hiram could get out of the girl was her sister's name and the fact that she had not worked for Fashion 85 for very long. It was fairly obvious that the girl should be contacted and sent home as soon as possible but Hiram did not know which department she worked in. Eventually, by tracing through the files, the girl was contacted and sent home. Her head of department was informed of the situation on the internal telephone and the girl was given leave of absence. Everything worked out well in the end but Hiram decided that a card index system would save a lot of valuable time should a similar situation occur again. It also occurred to him that some extra information could be included. He would then have all the vital information at his finger tips.

1   Design a card suitable for Hiram Clarke's card index system (show what information you could include).
2   In what order would you store the cards?
3   The department each person works in is very important. How could you make each department's record cards stand out?
4   What extra information could be included on the cards?
5   Why didn't Hiram Clarke just have a list of names typed with the information written beside each name?

Documents

The main method of collecting and storing data is by means of a document. Data may be recorded in printed form and then used or stored in some way. Documents may be divided into three main groups.

1   **Source documents** are used for the initial recording of data which will usually be processed into some other form before it is used. An example of this is a clock card which records the arrival and departure times of employees. The data on a clock card is used as a basis for working out payroll information.
2   **Intermediate documents** are usually used for collecting data from service documents and providing summaries from which reports can be

written. The clock cards can be used to provide departmental summaries of man-hours. This might be important when analysing overtime working in each department, for example.

3 **Reports** are the final usable information which may be stored or presented to management to allow some action to be taken. It may also be used to convey information from one company to another, as in the case of statements of accounts which give details of payments made and outstanding debts over a period of time.

Forms design—a useful checklist

Relevant information

Has this been obtained:

1 from all users inside and outside the organisation?
2 about methods of completion, eg pen, pencil, typewriter?
3 about the office operations associated with the document, eg filing, sorting, copying, summarising?
4 about other related documents?
5 from completed specimens of the form?
6 about working conditions?
7 about figures of use, errors, queries, percentage and quality of replies, cost?

The heading

Can this be simplified:

1 by making the title describe the form, thus helping recognition?
2 by changing the position and typesize of the name of the department?
3 by removing any words or figures which give it a cluttered-up appearance?

Instructions

1 Is the wording and layout designed to reduce instructions to a minimum?
2 Have general points been classified and grouped in one place to help understanding?
3 Have all notes about entries been placed close to the entry space?
4 Have footnotes been eliminated and turning over reduced to a minimum?

The wording

1   Are there any words which are not essential?
2   Is there any jargon or departmental terminology which needs to be eliminated?
3   Is all the wording sufficiently clear so that doubt or queries will be avoided?
4   Would examples assist understanding and completion?
5   Has unnecessary officiousness and rudeness been avoided?

Layout

1   Is the layout simple?
2   Does it follow a logical order?
3   What aids would eliminate, reduce or simplify operations, such as reading, copying and typing, arithmetic, filing, sorting, reference, folding, progressing, interviewing, eg use of the words *office use only* over appropriate sections.
4   Has the best use been made of space?
5   Is the size appropriate:

a for all operations;
b for the printer;
c for other documents with which the form may have to be used;
d for storage?

6   Do the working conditions suggest special layout requirements, eg making up in pads, facilities for quick entries, easy carbon extraction?

Material

1   Do the working conditions necessitate any special material?
2   What quality is needed:

a for writing;
b for handling?

3   Have storage requirements been considered?

Specification

What instructions are necessary for the printer in respect of:

1   quality of paper?
2   typographic requirements?
3   colours of paper and ink?
4   special requirements, eg size, folding, punching, perforating, registrations?
5   proofs and delivery date?

The efficient recording of data on documents is governed by the design of the form. It has to be easy to fill in the form, and aids to completing the documents must be given or the forms will not be completed correctly, if at all. The production, distribution and collection of the forms has to be thought about as carefully as the design of the forms.

Even before the form is produced the method of production has some bearing on the final design. Certain coloured inks will not photocopy so they cannot be used on forms which are to be reproduced in this way. Documents sent from one company to another should be of high quality and this may involve expensive printing techniques, especially if coloured inks are required.

The size and type of print required is important when deciding on the method of production. Headings and titles may be required in a certain size and style only available with special techniques. The size of type may also be important in allowing the correct amount of information to be contained on a page. Everyone is aware of the problems caused by small print which is often used on legal documents and has a reputation for hiding items of information which people are not supposed to read too carefully! The title lines, print and layout should be chosen to make the document look attractive.

Choosing the wording on a form is a very difficult task. It should give instructions on how to fill in the form in a clear, concise and unambiguous way. Examples can often be used to make the instructions more explicit. Colours or shading may be helpful to the person completing the form but these should be used with care; many people are colour blind and have difficulty in distinguishing between colours.

The people who design forms often work in offices where they have desks on which to rest while writing down information. Many of the people who complete such forms are not so fortunate. In some cases the need to complete forms has to be kept to an absolute minimum; for example, the mechanics in the Fashion 85 Transport Department often have greasy hands and a messy workbench and it is unreasonable to expect them to wash their hands and move to a desk every few minutes to fill in forms. Card or heavy paper should be used for forms which have to be used in this type of situation and the minimum amount of writing should be required.

Many forms are completed by people who only have a clipboard for a desk. To make such forms easier to complete the writing should be required on the left-hand side of the form. The reason for this layout is that most people are right-handed and this entails holding the clipboard in the left hand while resting the right hand on the clipboard. In such a situation it is especially important to keep the amount of writing to a minimum. One way this can be achieved is to print as much information as possible on the forms, leaving the user to fill in numbers, preferably in boxes, or put ticks against a choice of answers.

Exercise 7

1   Frank Stamper has decided to change the method of issuing stationery. He has decided to issue stock only on receipt of a requisition form signed by the head of department. The first attempt at producing a requisition was a bit of a failure, as you can see below.

FASHION 85 **Stationery requisition** **Department: (Delete as necessary) T/A/S/P/O/Pr** Date:		
Item Quantity		
Signature of Head of Department		

Stationery requisition form (first design)

a What is wrong with the form?
b Carefully design a form suitable for obtaining stationery for the office.
c Fill in your form to requisition ten blue biros and two reams of A4 plain typing paper for the Accounts Department.

2   Obtain from the Post Office an application form to relicence a motor vehicle and an application form for a driving licence.

a Write down the code numbers of these forms.
b Are these forms perfect? If not, how could they be improved?
c Fill in the application form for a driving licence.

3   You want to keep a check on your spending over a month. Decide on suitable headings under which you can describe items of expenditure, eg clothes, food, bus fares, etc. form

Design a form suitable for recording the amount spent on each of these items over a four-week period.

Mark off areas of the form in which you can work out the total expenditure on each item over the four weeks and areas for the average weekly expenditure on each item.

Fill in your form and work out the totals and averages.

4 Visit a library and examine the card index catalogue.

a Why are there two different types of catalogue?

b Write down the details recorded on a typical entry on the author's index.

Punched cards

A punched card is a simple method of recording information as a pattern of holes in a card. Several methods of using cards are available, some of which require expensive equipment. Until recently this method of recording information was the most popular method of getting information into a computer system. It was for this reason that 'standard' punch cards were designed. This meant that cards could be used with equipment made by many different manufacturers.

A standard punch card

The standard punch card (see above) is 19 cm long and 8 cm high. It has spaces (or columns) for 80 characters which are recorded as small rectangular holes punched through one or more of the 12 rows available. Numbers are recorded by a single hole in the appropriate row numbered 0 to 9. The number 157, for example, consists of a hole in row 1 of the first column, a hole in row 5 of the second column and a hole in row 7 of the third column.

Letters, punctuation marks and other symbols may be recorded using a combination of holes in the ten numeric rows or by using the numeric rows in conjunction with the two rows at the top of the card, which are usually called the **zone rows**. The letter A could then be recorded by a hole in row 12 and a hole in row 1 in the same column.

Early punched card equipment put each hole in the card separately. The operators had to learn the punching code for each character and then use a key pad, numbered 1 to 12, to actually punch the correct rows. On later machines a keyboard like that on a typewriter was linked to the punching equipment. When a key was pressed the machine automatically produced the correct code as well as printing the character on the top of the card.

The advantage of this medium over the card index for a lot of data is that the punched card can be produced or read by a machine. Many different machines have been developed to deal with cards, such as the following:

1 **Card punches** record the information on cards. A Data Processing Department may employ several girls who transfer information from forms to punched cards. Alternatively, information may be transferred to punched cards from a computer.

2 **Card readers** read the data from the cards and transfer it to a computer.

3 **Interpreters** print the characters which are recorded on the card. Most modern card punches print the characters along the top of the card as well as punching the holes. However, older machines and those which produce output from a computer do not have this facility, which means that they are difficult for people to read. In such a situation the interpreter may be used to print the contents of the cards.

4 **Sorters** sort cards into some known order. They can also be used to find cards which contain a required piece of information. In the past these were very useful machines but they are gradually disappearing because of the increasing use of small computer systems.

5 **Verifiers** are used to check the information punched on the cards. When machines are being used to speed up data processing operations it is very important that the data is correct. Any mistakes will be processed at the same speed as correct data. To avoid errors it is important to build as many checks into a system as possible. One possible source of errors is when information is being copied from source documents to punched cards. To help avoid these errors most systems verify the cards. A girl uses a card punch to record the data on the cards. When she has finished she passes the completed cards and the source documents to another girl who operates a verifier. The second girl punches exactly the same information on the same cards. If the verifier detects any differences between the holes already punched in the cards and the holes that it is making in the cards then the keyboard locks, telling the operator that a mistake has been made. The operator then hand punches a replacement card and re-verifies it.

A lot of this type of equipment is now being replaced by small, relatively cheap computer systems.

The data is organised on punched cards in a similar way to a card index. Each card is divided into a series of fields, each one relating to a single piece of data. All of the pieces of data relating to the same item form a **record**. This is usually a single card (see below). All of the cards relating to the same items form a **punched card file**.

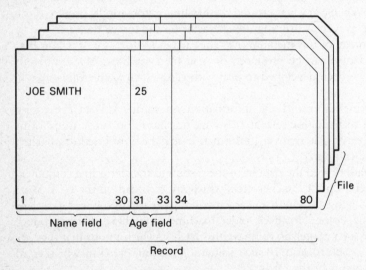

A punch card with a name field and an age field

It is usually convenient to have each **field** on the card of a fixed length. The **name field** for example is 30 characters long even though Joe Smith takes up only 9 characters. This has several benefits. The **age field** will always start in column 31. When a machine reads this card it does not understand what it reads. If we want a machine to pick out the names of all of the people over 20 years old we must tell it to read columns 31 and 32. This could not be done if we punched the age directly after the name as this would mean that the *age field* would be in a different position on each card.

Another advantage of fixed-length fields is that they speed up the method of punching. On most punching machines a plugboard is available which can be programmed. A plug may be put in to represent a column. In this case a plug could be put into column 31. After typing the name a special key called a **skip** would cause the punch to jump automatically to column 31 to allow the age to be input. This saves the operator time because she doesn't have to move along column by column. Plugs can be put into the plugboard for the

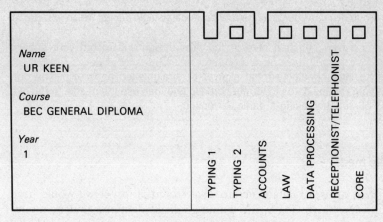

A punch card used to record subject options at college

start of each field. The plugboard can be used to carry out other processes automatically. Cards may be copied or perhaps the more useful part of a card may be copied allowing the operator to complete the card manually.

It is not always necessary to use expensive equipment to record and process punched cards. Colleges often have to be able to find out the names of people doing a particular set of options. (In school it is useful to be able to find out who is doing particular subjects.) This may be done using a simple punched card system.

The card above is an example of the one used to record U R Keen's subject options. The left-hand side records information about U R Keen; the right-hand side records the options available on the course.

Holes are punched in the same position on each card above the subject options available. It is important that each subject, whether studied or not, has a hole punched. The subjects which are *not* studied have slots cut out from the hole to the top of the card. All of the cards belonging to students on the same course form a *card file* and the holes should line up when the cards are held together. To find the names of students studying a particular subject option the cards are held together and a long needle is passed through the hole for the required option. When the needle is lifted up the cards belonging to those students taking the option will remain on the needle whilst the remaining cards will drop off. Information can then be read from the cards on the needle.

Exercise 8

1 Obtain a piece of thin card approximately 15 cm by 8 cm.
2 Design a punched card on which you can record your own subject options.

3 As a group discuss your designs and produce a single design which you can all use.
4 Produce a new punched card to the new design and record your subject options.
5 Obtain a long needle (a meat skewer or straightened paper clip may do). Combine your groups cards to form a card file and then use the needle to remove the cards of students taking a particular option.

Magnetic media

If every item of useful data generated was stored on paper we would have very serious problems. The world would gradually disappear under a mountain of paper. The main problems with paper are that it is expensive and bulky to store. When the data on it has been used it is thrown away (some paper is recycled but that is a relatively expensive business and the resulting paper is generally of a low quality). Quite often the data has to be transferred to a machine of some sort for processing and the original document is then useless.

In some applications paper is not suitable for recording data because of the conditions under which it is collected. Alternative methods of recording data have to be made available. One of these is to store information magnetically on recording tape or discs. The entertainments industry has been doing this for a long time, producing music and then storing it on tape or cassette. Whenever you play a recording you are reproducing recorded data.

The type of data which may be stored on magnetic tape varies. A surveyor may use a portable cassette machine to record measurements on a building site or a computer may record programs or the number of tins of beans on the shelf in the local supermarket, both in a similar fashion.

A proportion of this information is understandable to humans but much of it is recorded by one machine to be played back to another and is only understandable to the machines. A computer program would not mean a great deal to a person listening to it but sounds sensible to a computer and enables it to get on with its job. Once the data has been used by the machine and processed the tape can be used over and over again and it is far easier to store the tape cassette than several hundred sheets of paper.

With some calculating machines it is possible to use a combination of written data and magnetically stored data. A small computer may be used which allows information to be typed on to a special card (**magnetic stripe card**). At the same time as the information is printed on the card it is also stored invisibly as a series of magnetic patterns on a strip of recording tape along the edge of the card. The computer can then use this magnetic data to carry out calculations and the answers can be produced under the control of the computer, either on the magnetic strip or printed on the card so that the operator can read them.

NCR microfiche reader

Collection of data recording media

An increasingly common method of recording data magnetically is to use a disc of coated plastic (like recording tape), about the same size as a small single record. These are called **floppy discs** and are mainly used in small computer systems for storing programs and data. A very large amount of data can be stored on each disc and the computer can quickly read any required section of it.

While it is often very useful to use magnetic media for storing data there are disadvantages. Special equipment is required to record and read it and if something happens to the tape or disc all the data may be lost for ever.

Ledger cards

An Accounts Department often has a filing system which is geared to its own special needs. This entails recording, in columns, details of items bought and sold and their prices. Simple calculations have to be performed on the entries in these files and in some cases entries in one column have to be copied into other columns or even into other ledgers.

A convenient method of storing these ledger files is in the form of a card index. Accounting machines (a cross between a typewriter and a mechanical calculator) could then be used to record the entries on the card and perform the calculations. The carriage of many of these machines is often large enough to hold two cards. The machine can then be 'programmed' so that as the operator types in entries the machine automatically performs the calculation, prints the result in the appropriate column and if necessary adds the information to the other card on the machine.

The increasing use of computer systems means that the use of ledger cards and accounting machines is declining.

Microfilm

One of the major problems with modern data processing systems is the number of documents involved and the amount of paper which has to be stored. This storage problem can be eased if the documents are made smaller and one way of doing this is to take a photograph of them. Using microfilm a sheet of paper can be reduced to a piece of film 2.4 cm by 3.6 cm or even less. A typical filing cabinet could hold many hundred times more information on film than it does on paper.

Two problems then occur. Firstly, the documents have to be filmed. This can be done using microfilm cameras which operate rather like duplicating machines. The camera is loaded with a film magazine or cassette, the documents are loaded and the machine is switched on. The pages of the document are automatically fed, one at a time, through the machine and photographed. In some systems several pages of a document may be photographed on the same piece of film (15 cm by 10 cm); this is called **microfiche**.

An alternative method of obtaining documents in this form is to have the output from a computer system fed directly to a machine which prints it straight on to the microfilm. With this type of output no paper document need be produced at all. This system is known as **COM** (computer output on microfilm).

The second problem with microfilm is that the print is too small to read. Having produced documents small enough to solve the storage problem it seems that they will be of little use. Two solutions exist to this problem. The better solution is to use microfilm readers. The microfilm is inserted into a device which looks like a television and a full-size image of the document is projected on to the screen, making it easy to read. The alternative and less desirable system is to put the microfilm through a machine which prints the contents back on to paper. This allows the microfilm to be read, but produces a storage problem again.

Microfilm has its problems and is only useful in certain applications. The equipment is very expensive both for reading and producing microfilm. However, this can be offset against the cost of storing large quantities of documents. One of the areas where microfilm has a very high advantage when compared to paper documents is when information has to be sent by post. Catalogues which may run into several hundred pages may change every few months. If they are produced on microfilm the savings in postal costs can be enormous when you consider that a single piece of film may contain a minimum of twelve pages.

Exercise 9

1 Design a poster to illustrate as many different ways of recording data as you can find. Use actual specimens of recorded data where possible but if this is not practical then pictures may be used to show different methods. Examples of the type of material you may like to include are punched cards and paper tape. Do not forget that items like bus tickets and library tickets contain recorded data.

2 Use *The Post Office Directory* (or visit the Post Office) to find the maximum number of A4 pages that can be sent in the UK using second-class post (you will have to weigh some paper to enable you to work this out). Assuming that 24 pages on microfilm weigh the same as one A4 sheet of paper, how many document pages on microfilm could be sent for the same price?

Assignment 4

The Westpool College of Further Education Students' Association has decided to hold a 'charity week' to raise funds for the local hospital. Each course in the college has to organise an activity which will make money. Engineering students are servicing domestic appliances for a small fee and secretarial students are offering a typing service. The Data Processing Department have decided that they will run a *dating service*. For a small fee students will be given the name of their ideal partner. This service breaks down into four main sections.

1　Collect the data from the students.
2　Organise the data for processing.
3　Process the data.
5　Distribute the results.

Data collection

After group discussions it was decided that the best way to collect the data would be to design some **data capture** forms. These could then be filled in by the students and returned to the Data Processing Section with the appropriate fee. Soon it became apparent that two different forms would be required if the system was to be kept as simple as possible. The male students would fill in a form on which they would give their name and course. They would then complete a section which described their physical appearance, hobbies and interests. The girls' form would be similar except that they would describe their ideal boyfriend.

One of the students suggested that the quickest method of processing the information would be to use punched cards. This meant that the forms would have to be designed so that students could answer 'yes' or 'no' to a series of questions about appearance and interests. The names and courses could be written on the cards so this would not cause any problems.

You have been nominated by the students' association to help to organise this project.

1　Write down a list of items which you think adequately describes physical appearance and personality, eg:

Height　　　　5' 3"
Hair colour　　Brown
etc

2　Compare your list with others in your group and obtain a 'standard' set of items which you can all use. Each item may be divided into several choices and your list may start like this:

Height	4' 6"–5' 0"
	5' 1"–5' 6"
	5' 7"–6' 0"
	Over 6' 0"
Hair colour	Fair
	Brown
	Black
	Other

3 A start has been made on the forms which will be used for collecting the male data but unfortunately the girl responsible for this section of the project is unable to finish it (she has moved away from the area). Make a copy of the form on page 36 (on an A4 sheet) and complete it. It would be useful if you could keep the number of choices down to below 30.

4 A similar form is required for the girls' data. The data items will be identical but the 'M1' at the top of the form will be replaced by 'F1' and the instruction line says: 'Please tick boxes which apply to your ideal boyfriend.' Design the forms and have copies of both forms made (about ten of each should be sufficient).

5 Ask your friends and colleagues to fill in the forms.

Questions

1 Why should the code change from M1 to F1 on the second form?

2 How can you make sure that the two forms can be easily identified so that students do not fill in the wrong form?

3 When you allow only a limited number of choices for each item the person filling in the form may not be able to find an item which is appropriate. How could this situation be avoided (or at least improved)?

Data preparation

The next stage in processing the data is to transfer it from the forms to suitably designed punched cards. Along the bottom of the card is an area in which the name and course can be written. The main part of the card is divided into columns. Each column is the equivalent of a box on the data collection form. A hole is punched near the top of *each* column.

Whenever a student has ticked a box on the form a groove is cut in the same column on his punched card, from the top of the card to the punched hole. This is repeated until each of the students has a punched card to match the form. The two sets of cards are separated into a boys' card file and girls' card file. Processing consists of comparing each girl's card in turn with the

WESTPOOL COLLEGE OF FURTHER EDUCATION

DATING SERVICE

Name ....

Course ....

Please tick boxes which you feel best apply **to you**

HEIGHT　　　Under 5'0" ☐
　　　　　　5'1"– 5'6" ☐
　　　　　　5'7"– 6'0" ☐
　　　　o　 Over 6'0" ☐

HAIR COLOUR　Fair ☐
　　　　　　　Brown ☐
　　　　　　　Black ☐
　　　　　　　Other ☐

Incomplete design of form for collection of data

complete file of boys' cards and finding the boy's card which is the closest match with that of the girl.

1　Collect together the boys' file. Place the first girl's card on the front of the boys' file. Push a needle (or long wire) through the first choice on the card. *Remember that you have cut grooves out of the cards to indicate the choices made.* When you lift up the needle all of the cards which do not match should remain on the needle and all of the matching cards should drop off. Collect up the cards which matched and write down the names of the matching boys.
2　Put all of the boys' cards together again and repeat the first stage for the

next choice on the same girl's card. Keep doing this until all of that girl's choices have been tested. The name which has been written down the most times belongs to the boy who most closely matches the girl's choice and the number of times the name occurs gives the number of items which matched.

3 Repeat the process for all of the girls in the file and record each girl, the corresponding boy and the number of items on which they matched.

Questions

1 Why not take the group of cards belonging to the boys who matched on the first item and see if they match on the second and so on? At the end you should only have one card left that will belong to the boy who matches best. This would require fewer comparisons and no writing would be required until the end.

2 The method of making a list of boys' names at each stage is not very efficient. Can you design a better method of recording the results at each stage of testing?

3 Two sets of cards are used in this system. What can you do to make it easy to differentiate between them?

Distributing results

The final stage of this project is to get the results back to the people who have taken part in the scheme. The actual method employed will depend upon the organisation in which it is run. This is very much a problem with the present scheme. One suggestion is to print cards containing the name and course of the girl and the name and course of the corresponding boy and then distribute the cards to the people concerned, but more efficient methods may be available.

1 Design and produce a card that can be given to each individual in the scheme giving the name of their matched partner.

2 Decide on the best method of distributing these results.

3 Distribute the results of your system.

Questions

1 As a result of your system have all of the boys and all of the girls been matched? If not what are you going to do about those without a partner?

2 Has one boy been matched with more than one girl and if so what are you going to do about it?

3 In this system the girls have chosen their ideal boyfriends but the boys have had no choice. To change the system so that the boys have a choice as well is not as simple as it may appear. Think carefully about the system and explain what changes would have to be made.

4 It is possible to work out how closely the girls matched the boys and express this as a percentage. This figure is worked out as follows:

$$\% \text{ match} = \frac{\text{number of items which match} \times 100}{\text{total number of items}}$$

Work out the percentage match for each girl in the system.

The Westpool College Charity Week was a great success and the local hospital was very grateful. One or two students who had taken part in the dating system were grateful too.

4 Errors

Everybody has heard of people getting bills for £0.00 and refunds from a company of 1p which came in an envelope with a first class stamp. These mistakes are usually blamed on a computer. This seems to suggest that only machines make mistakes whereas in fact nearly all errors in a system will have been made by people at one stage or another.

It is impossible to eliminate all of the errors from any system which involves human beings. You have only to look at the number of false alarms at American missile sites to see that no matter how careful you are mistakes will still be made. The armed forces minimise the effect of mistakes by having complicated back-up systems designed to detect errors and correct them before anything serious occurs. In commerce and industry the consequences of people making mistakes may not be as serious as in the armed forces but any mistakes made are bad for business.

Mistakes cost money. Apart from the money that might be lost as a direct result of the error, eg money misplaced or arithmetic errors on bills, people will have to be paid for the time taken to correct the error. If a company makes lots of mistakes its customers lose faith and go to a more reliable firm. This means a loss of business, which no company can afford.

The obvious answer is for people to be more careful and to check their work, but this is not really sufficient. Therefore systems have to be designed to make errors easier to detect.

Types of error

Errors can usually be divided into five different types. All of these are avoidable and most can be detected by building some form of test into the system.

Transcription

Whenever data has to be transferred from one document to another errors are likely to be introduced. The most common reason for this is the inability of one person to read another person's writing accurately. Certainly characters can easily be copied incorrectly because they are similar to other characters, eg I is read as 1 and 1 becomes I, s and 5 may be confused, zero and O may be confused.

Data processing installations may use certain rules to help avoid these errors, eg I is always written with bars at the top and bottom (topped and tailed), zero may be written as Ø and S may be written as S̲.The rules, however, vary from company to company.

Transposition

This type of error is very common with numeric data. It may also be quite difficult to detect in many cases. When writing down numbers it is very easy to change the order of digits. In this way the number 5134 becomes 5314. If the number is to be used as a code it may be possible to build in a method of checking it (see the panel on self checking numbers). Otherwise it may be possible to detect the error when arithmetic checking is carried out.

Arithmetic

Everybody, no matter how clever they are at arithmetic, makes mistakes with figures at one time or another. The use of devices like electronic calculators may help to reduce these errors but it is very easy to press the wrong button. Many people have the feeling that calculators are infallible and they believe any answer they get out of one of these machines. A large number of arithmetic errors could be avoided if the people using the machines stopped for a second and said, 'Is the answer reasonable?' If the answer is 'No' then the calculation should be rechecked.

Data out of date

Quite often prices and styles of goods offered change frequently. Obviously under these circumstances it is important that the data is the most up to date available. While charging last year's prices may be good for customer relations it could be financial suicide for a company. This again may cause errors which are difficult to detect. The person processing the data may be unaware that more recent data is available.

In this particular case it is probably the job of management to ensure that all employees are notified of changes in the data with which they are involved. This notification may be in the form of memos or additions to catalogues, price lists and so on.

Loss of data

This is perhaps the most serious form of error. Data may be lost for many reasons, the two most common being misplacing of forms or, in the case of computerised systems, machine failure.

Self checking numbers

These are code numbers which have a **check digit** added in order to provide some method of discovering whether they are valid or not. Several methods of calculating check digits are available.

Method 1—mod 11

Suppose the original code number is 3155. Carry out the following operations.

1 Divide the number by 11:

   3155/11 = 286, remainder **9**

2 Join the remainder on to the original code number:

   31559

3 Always use 31559 as the code number.

   If the original code had been 3156 then the remainder when the value was divided by 11 would be 10. This cannot be represented as a single digit so the special code × is used.

   3156/11 = 286 remainder **10**

so the code number becomes **3156×**.

Method 2—weighted mod 11

An improved check digit can be produced by first multiplying the digits of the code number by a sequence of numbers called **weights**. A weighted mod 11 check digit can be produced as follows.

   Suppose the code is 3155 and the weights are 5, 4, 3, 2. Multiply each digit by its weight:

Code	3	1	5	5
Weights	5	4	3	2
Product	15	4	15	10

Add together the products:

   15 + 4 + 15 + 10 = 44

Divide the answer by 11:

   44/11 = 4, remainder **0**

Join remainder on to code:

   31550

Method 3—ISBN

Every book published has its own unique code number. This is known as the
ISBN or International Standard Book Number. The book *People at Work*,
for example, has the following code:

0	273	01316	5
Country of origin	Publisher's code no	Class and code of book	Check digit

The check digits are worked out as follows:

Code	0	2	7	3	0	1	3	1	6
Weights	10	9	8	7	6	5	4	3	2

Products   0 18 56 21 0 5 12 3 12
Sum of products = 0 + 18 + 56 + 21 + 0 + 5 + 12 + 3 + 12 = 127
Mod 11 value = 127/11 = 11, remainder 6
Check digit = 11 − 6 = **5**

Note that this method includes an extra stage: the remainder is subtracted
from 11 before becoming the check digit.

Testing numbers

To test code numbers for validity write down the code **without** the check
digit. Work out what the check digit should be and then compare it with the
original value. This is often done automatically by computer programs.

If the data has been copied before the original is lost it is possible that the
loss will only result in the expensive and time consuming task of finding the
copy of the original data and duplicating any processing which may have
already been carried out. Where no copy exists the situation may be far more
serious. For this reason most companies find it prudent to make copies of
documents.

Exercise 10

1 The code number S105 has to be copied on to a series of forms. This number
was not written down very clearly in the first place and every time it was copied
mistakes were made.

a Write down as many different versions of this code as you can think of.

b How could the code have been written in the first place to avoid some or all of
the wrong versions?

2 A set of data was transferred from one form to another by a girl whose mind
was obviously on something else at the time. Copy out the table below and say
what type of error has occurred.

Original	Copy	Error
S256	5256	
3756	3765	
5016	5O16	
DEF715S	DFE715S	
RHS327×	RH5327×	
OS245	0S245	
OS245	O5245	
OS245	OS425	

3 Mistakes are often made when arithmetic has to be carried out. Check the following sums to see if they are correct. If mistakes have been made see if you can find out where they have occurred.

a 5 × £3.72 = £18.50
b 4 × £2.16 = £8.46
c 429.36 − 187.24 = 342.12
d 625.23 + 127.02 = 752.43
e 1000 − 62.32 = 1063.68

Avoiding and detecting errors

Many methods of avoiding and detecting errors are available. Most of them involve extra work. In some cases the work is duplicated but it is still worth while avoiding the problems that mistakes can lead to. When computers are used for data processing many of the checks can be written into the programs that they use; the checks are therefore carried out automatically. The main checks which can be carried out in data processing systems fall into the following two categories.

Verifying

This is usually used when entering data into a computer system. Data is typed in by one person (perhaps to be transferred to punched cards). A different person then enters the same data and the two sets are compared. If there are any differences between the two sets then one of the operators has probably made a mistake and corrections can be made.

The idea is that in general two people will not make the same mistake. This situation is improved if the second person cannot actually see what the first person has typed. This can be done using special machines which store the information typed by the first person in a 'machine readable' form. The machine automatically compares the original data and the typed data and signals any errors.

Check digits

To avoid errors of transcription and transposition it is possible to use code numbers which have a built in test that makes sure that they have been written down properly. These tests usually involve carrying out some arithmetic operation on the codes to give a value called a **check digit** (see the panel on self checking numbers). This value then becomes part of the code number. Whenever the code is used a simple mathematical check can be carried out to ensure that the number has been written down correctly.

Many types of self checking numbers can be used but a company generally chooses one method and uses it all the time. These codes cannot be used for code numbers which have to follow each other in a consecutive sequence.

The generation of the codes would initially be carried out by a machine. The checking of code numbers can also be done automatically by machine.

Exercise 11

1 The order number 3056 was copied from an order form to an invoice and a despatch note. Unfortunately it became 30S6 on the invoice and 3065 on the despatch note. Explain what has happened in each case and say what steps may be taken to avoid or detect these errors.

2 Calculate a mod 11 check digit for 3056.

3 Use a 5, 4, 3, 2 weighting and mod 11 to find check digits for the following:

a 1235

b 2613

c 3522

4 Use the last digit of each of the following as a mod 11 check digit (no weightings have been used) and find out if the codes are correct:

a 237567

b 13496×

c 32×

d 1590

e 795832

f 23492172

5 The following numbers have weighted mod 11 check digits added. The weights used are 5, 4, 3, 2. Test the code numbers to see if they are valid:

a 63517

b 45371

c 31549

d 91728

e 97317

6   Fashion 85 recently ordered some books for the technical library. You are to check the ISBNs to see if they are correct.

a 0 907 21100 3

b 0 408 00182 8

c 0 140 5039 7

Assignment 5

1   Using the extracts from the Fashion 85 catalogue (see Appendix 3) and the customer file (see Appendix 2) check through the order form on page 46. Whenever you come across an error make a note of it. Say what type of error it is and if possible explain how the error may have occurred.

2   Some of the items on the order may not have incorrect code numbers and prices but may still contain errors. What checks can you make on such items to see if an error **may** have occurred? Write down one such item from the order form.

3   Write out a 'corrected' version of the order. In the case of some of the errors you may have to make a guess at the correct version.

4   What would you do as an employee of Fashion 85 if you received an order like this one to process?

5   What steps could you take as an employee of Guys & Dolls to make sure that an order like this one was never sent out?

6   Can you think of any extra costs which might be involved in processing an order with errors in it rather than a correct one? If you can, make a list of them.

Further checks for errors

The number of methods of making sure that data is not lost or altered are increasing all the time as people realise how important this area is to the well being of an organisation. As well as the methods already examined there are many others.

Denham House, Weavers Way
WESTPOOL Cleveland CV3 5DW

Telephone Westpool (0937) 47632 3 4
Telex 152773
Telegraphic Address DENWAY WESTPOOL

FASHION 85 LIMITED

VAT Reg No 421 4647 61R

ORDER

Order No **S1**

Date **29 February 19-1**

GUYS & DOLLS
24 Wimborne Road
Gateshead
Tyne & Wear

Delivery to:

By

Special Instructions

Quantity	Ref No	Description	Unit Price £
12	E3276	Dress Size 12	13.75
12	E3276	Dress Size 14	13.75
10	E3277	Dress Size 10	11.00
100	E3120	Tabard Size 14	5.75
5	B1677	Slacks flared Size 20	45.00
2	B1628	Culotte Cream Size 13	3.75
2	MD0S	Jacket Size 10	6.25
10pr	L977	Sportsocks 8½ - 9½	7.50
10pr	L979	Socks 10 - 11	7.00

Authorised by:

Order form

Hash and control totals

In this method you add up all of the numeric values on a form and write down the total. Whenever the values are transferred to other forms the person that carries out the transfer adds all the values together again. The new total is compared with the original. If they are the same then the values have probably been written down correctly; otherwise an error has probably occurred.

When the values that are added together have some real meaning (amounts of money on order forms, say) these are called **control totals**. In some cases the values used give a result that is totally meaningless except for error checking. These are called **hash totals**.

Consider the dating service run at the Westpool College of Further Education. Data collected on the forms had to be transferred to punched cards, but it was difficult to check whether the information on the cards was the same as the original data on the forms. If the total number of ticks had been counted and checked against the number of holes punched in the cards that would have given a simple method of checking the punching. The total for the number of ticks is in itself fairly meaningless. This would have been a **hash total**.

Batch control

When lots of forms have to be dealt with it is quite easy for one or more to get lost. Obviously if this happens the results could be disastrous. If the processing is uncontrolled then the lost forms may not be detected until it is too late. To prevent the likelihood of this happening a close control has to be kept on the number of documents being used at any one time. One method of doing this is to batch the documents by collecting them into groups or **batches**.

Each group has a special document attached to the front called a **batch control form**. In its simplest version this would contain a number relating to this particular collection of documents (**batch number**) and the number of documents included (**number in batch**).

A space would be provided for the person processing the forms to sign. This would show that all of the documents in the batch had been dealt with. In this way each person dealing with the set of forms knows how many documents there should be and can easily keep a check to make sure that none go missing.

Some batch control forms are more complicated and may contain some further information such as hash or control totals. This gives more opportunities to check that the processing has been carried out correctly.

Balances

A useful method of recording data is in the form of a table. Quite often the rows and columns of the table have to be added up. This could result in errors in arithmetic. One way of checking whether a mistake has occurred is to add up the totals for each of the rows and the totals for each of the columns and compare the two figures. If they are different then a mistake has probably occurred.

For example, look at the production table below. The rows of this table indicate the number of items produced by each person. *Total 1* gives the total production for each person. The columns of the table give the daily production figures and the figures in *Total 2* give the daily production totals. The total number of items produced during the week are the same whether you add up the number produced by each person during the week or the number produced each day. This means that if all of the values in column *Total 1* are added together the value should be the same as that obtained by adding together all of the values in row *Total 2*. If the two totals do not agree then an error (probably in arithmetic) has occurred and this must be found and corrected.

Production figures

Week no ....

Name	*Mon*	*Tues*	*Wed*	*Thurs*	*Fri*	*Total 1*
Smith J	218	220	200	213	222	1 073
Jones D	200	216	95	175	105	791
Makeit I	213	214	200	190	220	1 037
Potter T	224	210	202	200	213	1 049
Fixit J	210	199	212	199	216	1 036
Mender T	205	204	256	206	202	1 073
Total 2	1 270	1 263	1 165	1 183	1 178	6 059

Signed ....

Production table

Exercise 12

The Transport Department of Fashion 85 keep a check on the mileage covered by each of their cars on a monthly basis. Each week the number of miles covered by every car is recorded in a table. At the end of the month the figures are added up. The rows of the table tell Roland Wheeler how many miles each car has covered during the month and the columns give him the total weekly mileage for the cars. At the end of the month when the totals are worked out they are balanced to make sure that no errors have occurred. Here is a typical form:

MILEAGE REPORT   Month ....

Registration no	Week number					Total 1
	1	2	3	4	5	
PQR 537W	123	185	234	95	13	
XYZ 765W	256	234	450	123	34	
PRS 345X	234	218	200	198	28	
YTR 564W	128	156	345	120	0	
PUT 56X	222	132	186	145	90	
XYZ 721X	165	222	123	203	20	
CVD 568X	304	316	342	214	22	
COX 211W	45	237	112	67	12	
UHF 333W	218	232	143	241	89	
DEF 522X	163	165	185	134	25	
Total 2						

Mileage chart

1 *a* For each car add up the mileages across the rows and put the answers in column *Total 1*.

   b For each week add up the mileages in the columns and put the answers in row *Total 2*.

   c Add up the totals in *Total 1* and write the value in the shaded box.

   d Add up the totals in *Total 2* and check that the answer is the same value as the number in the shaded box. If the two values do not agree you must check your arithmetic.

2 Design a batch control form for use within Fashion 85. This form should contain the *batch no, department name, number of documents contained in the batch,* *date* and the *signature* of the person putting the forms together. Certain applications may require a control total to be put on to the form. Include any other information which you think is important.

Denham House, Weavers Way
WESTPOOL Cleveland CV3 5DW

Telephone: Westpool (0937) 47632 3 4
Telex: 152773
Telegraphic Address: DENWAY WESTPOOL

FASHION 85 LIMITED

VAT Reg No 421 4647 61R

ORDER

Order No **66761**

Date **30th March 19-1**

Taylor's Dummy
Newcastle upon Tyne
Tyne & Wear

Delivery to:

By

Special Instructions

Quantity	Ref No	Description	Unit Price £
10	E3275	Trouser Suit Size 14	12.50
5	E3278	Jumpsuit Size 10	7.50
8	B1673	Slacks flared Size 18	3.30
8	B1678	Slacks flared Navy Size 20	4.50
8	B1681	Jeans Denim Blue Size 11	5.80
10	M002	Anorak, Sailing Orange Size M	4.80
10	D612	Kagooles Boys' Blue Size L	2.90
9	L980	Socks Double thick Grey Multi-fit	1.10
9	L980	Socks Double thick Black Multi-fit	1.10
10	B1678	Slacks flared Navy Size 22	4.50
5	B1680	Jeans Cord Camel Size 9	4.25
5	B1684	Culotte Cord Cream Size 13	4.25
5	M005	Jacket, Ski Cream Size 12	6.25
2	D612	Kagooles Boys' Blue Size M	2.90

Authorised by:

Assignment 6

As an office junior for Fashion 85 you find that from time to time you are on loan to other departments. On one such occasion you find that you are in the Sales Department helping to process orders. You are told that orders come in

---

Denham House, Weavers Way
WESTPOOL Cleveland CV3 5DW

Telephone Westpool (0937) 47632 3 4
Telex 152773
Telegraphic Address DENWAY WESTPOOL

FASHION 85 LIMITED

VAT Reg No 421 4647 61R

ORDER

Order No **61218**   Date **30th March 19-1**

Eunice Francis Modes   Delivery to:
Whitehaven
Cumbria   By

Special Instructions

Quantity	Ref No	Description	Unit Price £
25	E3276	Suit Size 16	13.75
10	E3279	Tabard Size 12	5.50
5	B1673	Slacks flared Brown Size 12	3.30
10	B1679	Jeans Cord Green Size 9	4.25
5	M002	Anorak, Sailing Size L	4.80
4	M007	Tracksuit Royal/White Size M	7.25
2	D612	Kagooles Boys' Orange Size M	2.90
2	D612	" " Blue Size M	2.90
1pr	L976	Sportsocks White/Blue trim 8½-9½	0.75
20prs	L977	Sportsocks " /Red trim 8½-9½	0.75
10prs	L978	Over knee White 8½-9½	0.65
5prs	L980	Socks Double Thick Fawn ⎫ Multifit	1.10
5prs	L980	" " " Black ⎭	1.10

Authorised by:

---

either on Fashion 85 order forms or as letters from companies. For convenience all orders should be on official Fashion 85 order forms.

Examine the orders on pages 50 to 57. If there are any which are not on the correct order forms then copy the details on to the appropriate document.

Denham House, Weavers Way
WESTPOOL Cleveland CV3 5DW

Telephone: Westpool (0937) 47632 3 4
Telex: 152773
Telegraphic Address: DENWAY WESTPOOL

FASHION 85 LIMITED

VAT Reg No 421 4647 61R

ORDER

Order No 76761

Date 30th March 19-1

Tillottson's Togs
Orpington
Kent

Delivery to:

By

Special Instructions

Quantity	Ref No	Description	Unit Price £
20	E3276	Suit Size 18	13.75
15	E3277	Dress Size 12	11.00
10	E3210	Tabard Grey Size 16	5.75
5	B1673	Slacks flared Size 14	3.30
8	B1679	Jeans Cord Green Size 15	4.25
6	B1684	Culotte Cord Size 13	4.25
7	M002	Anorak, Sailing Orange Size M	4.80
5	M004	Jacket, Ski Navy Size 20	6.50
5	M006	Jacket, Ski Green Size 10	6.50
5	M006	" " " Size 12	6.50
5	M008	Tracksuit Black/Orange Size M	7.25
6	D612	Kagooles Boys' Orange Size L	2.90
2	D612	" " Blue Size M	2.90
5prs	L978	Over knee White 8½-9½	0.65

Authorised by:

Denham House, Weavers Way
WESTPOOL Cleveland CV3 5DW

Telephone Westpool (0937) 47632 3 4
Telex 152773
Telegraphic Address DENWAY WESTPOOL

FASHION 85 LIMITED

VAT Reg No 421 4647 61R

ORDER

Order No **26463**

Date **10 March 19-1**

Don Lines
Gateshead
Tyne & Wear

Delivery to:

By **Rail**

Special Instructions

Quantity	Ref No	Description	Unit Price £
2 Doz	B1673	Slacks Brown Size 12	3.30
2 Doz	B1673	" " Size 14	3.30
1 Doz	B1679	Jeans Cord Green Size 9	4.25
1 Doz	B1679	Jeans Cord Size 13	4.25
1 Doz	M002	Anorak Orange Size S	4.80
1 Doz	M004	Ski Jackets Navy Size 16	6.50
1 Doz	M005	Ski Jackets Cream Size 14	6.25

Authorised by:

Denham House, Weavers Way
WESTPOOL Cleveland CV3 5DW

Telephone: Westpool (0937) 47632 3 4
Telex: 152773
Telegraphic Address: DENWAY WESTPOOL

FASHION 85 LIMITED

VAT Reg No 421 4647 61R

ORDER

Order No **26318**

Date **8 March 19-1**

Delivery to:

Eileen Dover
Hartlepool
Cleveland

By **Road**

Special Instructions

Quantity	Ref No	Description		Unit Price £
24	E3275	Trouser Suit	Size 12	12.50
			Size 14	12.50
			Size 16	12.50
24	L976	Sportsocks		0.75
10	B1684	Culotte	Size 13	4.25
			Size 15	4.25

Authorised by:

Denham House, Weavers Way
WESTPOOL Cleveland CV3 5DW

Telephone. Westpool (0937) 47632 3 4
Telex: 152773
Telegraphic Address: DENWAY WESTPOOL

FASHION 85 LIMITED

VAT Reg No 421 4647 61R

ORDER

Order No **27158**

Date **13th March 19-1**

Willie Golightly
Northallerton
North Yorks

Delivery to:

By

Delivery Van

Special Instructions

Quantity	Ref No	Description	Unit Price £
25	E3210	Tabard Grey Size 14	5.75
15	E3277	Dress Size 12	11.00
15	"	" Size 14	11.00
10	E3278	Jumpsuit Gold Size 10	7.50
10	E3278	" " Size 12	7.50
10	E3278	" " Size 14	7.50

Authorised by:

Denham House, Weavers Way
WESTPOOL Cleveland CV3 5DW

Telephone: Westpool (0937) 47632 3 4
Telex: 152773
Telegraphic Address: DENWAY WESTPOOL

FASHION 85 LIMITED

VAT Reg No 421 4647 61R

ORDER

Order No **15351**

Date **8th March 19-1**

Willie Golightly
Northallerton
North Yorks

Delivery to:

By

Special Instructions

Quantity	Ref No	Description		Unit Price £
2Doz	E3275	Trouser suit	Size 12	12.50
2Doz	E3275	" "	Size 14	12.50
6	E3279	Tabard	Size 10	5.50
6	E3279	Tabard	Size 14	5.50
5	B1673	Slacks	Size 12	3.30
5	B1673	Slacks	Size 16	3.30
5	B1674	"	Size 16	3.30
1Doz	B1679	Jeans	Size 11	4.25
1Doz	B1679	"	Size 15	4.25

Authorised by:

LONDON GIRL
59 Middleton Grange
WESTPOOL
Cleveland
Telephone: Westpool (0937) 62651
Telex: 543791

---

26 March 19-1
Fashion 85 Ltd
Denham House
Weavers Way
Westpool CV35DW

Dear Sirs
O/No 25368
Please have the following goods delivered to
our warehouse at the above address.

50   E3278   Jumpsuit, gold lurex, size 10 £7.50 each
65   B1679   Jeans, green cord, size 11 £4.25 each
70   B1681   "   denim blue, size 11 £5.80 "
50   B1692   Culotte cord skirt, size 9 £3.75 each
25   M003   Ski jackets, navy, size 10 £6.50 "
25   M005   "   "   cream, size 10 £6.25 "

An early delivery would be appreciated.

Yours faithfully
Heather Stephen
HEATHER STEPHEN (Ms)

Batch these forms together (fill in a batch control form (below) and clip it to the order form).

Denham House, Weavers Way
WESTPOOL Cleveland CV3 5DW

Telephone: Westpool (0937) 47632 3 4
Telex: 152773
Telegraphic Address: DENWAY WESTPOOL

FASHION 85 LIMITED

BATCH CONTROL

Date ....

Batch number ....

Number in batch ☐

Department ....

Checked by ....

(*This form may be reproduced if desired.*)

Check all of the details on the order forms against the extracts from the Fashion 85 catalogue and customer file (see Appendices 2 and 3). If the details are correct the orders can proceed to the next stage.

Complete invoices and despatch notes on pages 59 and 60, each in duplicate, for each order in the batch.

You now have a set of order forms which will be filed in your office, a set of invoices which will go to the Accounts Department and a set of despatch notes to go to the warehouse. Batch control forms should be filled in for each of these sets of documents.

While you are carrying out these procedures questions come to mind and you discuss these with the people around you. Write down the answers you might receive to the following questions (discuss the answers with the other members of your group).

1 How do you deal with orders that contain errors?
2 Why do you need to check the order details against the customer file?
3 If the customer has never ordered anything from Fashion 85 before his name will not appear on the customer file. What information will be required to enable you to add his name to the file?

Denham House, Weavers Way
WESTPOOL Cleveland CV3 5DW

Telephone: Westpool (0937) 47632 3 4
Telex: 152773
Telegraphic Address: DENWAY WESTPOOL

FASHION 85 LIMITED

VAT Reg No 421 4647 61R

INVOICE

Order No

Date

To:

Delivery to:

By

Invoice number

Quantity	Ref No	Description	Unit Price £	Total Price £

Authorised by

(This form may be reproduced if desired.)

Denham House, Weavers Way
WESTPOOL Cleveland CV3 5DW

Telephone: Westpool (0937) 47632 3 4
Telex 152773
Telegraphic Address: DENWAY WESTPOOL

FASHION 85 LIMITED

VAT Reg No 421 4647 61R

DESPATCH NOTE

Order No

Date

Delivery to:

By

Special Instructions

Quantity	Ref No	Description	Unit Price £	Total Price £

Authorised by

(*This form may be reproduced if desired.*)

4 Why are two copies required of the despatch notes and invoices?
5 Why are despatch notes and invoices different colours?
6 What will the Accounts Department do with the two copies of the invoice?
7 What is the purpose of the despatch note?

5 Data capture

Data is generated in vast quantities in all sorts of situations and, as we have already seen, it must be processed to provide useful information. This means that data is wild, so to speak, and must be tamed before it can be used.

The first step in this process is to capture the data. This is the term used to describe the act of recording data in some form. Filling in a form is an act of data capture. Ug and Og, the farmers who started the information explosion, may not have realised it at the time but when they cut notches in their tally sticks they were performing data capture.

Nowadays modern industrial and commercial organisations have to operate at great speed in order to remain efficient and competitive. The old fashioned methods of data capture by recording on forms are often too slow and have to be streamlined or replaced by automatic methods. Increasing use of computer systems means that data can be captured by a machine. The machine can then pass it on to a computer, which in turn processes it automatically and produces the information in a form suitable for people to use. In such cases the data is almost untouched by human hand from start to finish.

Data capture and shops

Justine Thyme decided that she would go on a shopping trip during her dinner hour. While browsing around the biggest department store in town she decided to buy the latest LP by The Scourge, the best group around at the moment (and besides she thought the lead singer was rather nice).

When she took the record to the cash point she was surprised to find that, instead of pushing buttons on the till, the girl picked up a pen attached to the till by a wire (see opposite, top). She passed the point of the pen across a label stuck on the record sleeve and the price appeared in a window of the till. The girl pressed a button on the till and the total amount for this sale appeared.

Justine paid the girl who put the record and the sales receipt in a bag. Later, when Justine examined the ticket she found that it told her exactly what she had bought, how much she had paid and the date (see opposite).

After buying the record Justine decided to pop into the boutique to buy a new skirt to wear at a party she was to attend at the weekend. She already had

A bar code pen

```
House of Fisher

    21/09/-1

Item        £

Record      4.99

Total       4.99
Cash        5.00
Change      0.01

Why not visit our cafe?
```

A receipt

an idea of what she wanted, but it did not take her long to decide that she didn't like it and she ended up buying something entirely different instead.

When she went to the desk to pay, the assistant ripped part of the price tag from the skirt and pushed it on to a spike by the till. Business must have been good because this was almost full. Having completed her shopping Justine had time to grab a quick sandwich and get back to work before the end of her lunch hour.

In her very short shopping trip Justine had discovered two types of data capture systems. The large department store obviously uses a computer to control stock and prices. The tills are called **point of sales terminals** (POS)

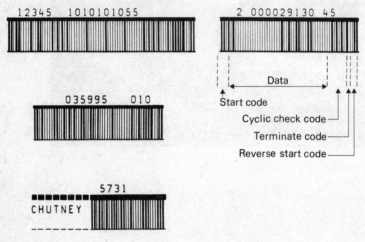

Bar code labels

and they are linked directly to a computer. On the record that she bought was a label which contained a bar code consisting of a series of thick and thin black lines (see above). When the tip of the 'pen' passed over this the code was sensed and the till passed the information to the computer.

At the computer the data is interpreted as a code for a particular item, complete with a check digit. The machine performs a quick calculation to see if it has read the code correctly and then it reads through all of the item codes stored in the memory to find the price of the item and the description. This information is then passed to the till which prints out the sales receipt.

While the till is carrying out this task the computer can carry out checks to see if the item sold is now out of stock. When the quantity in stock gets very low the computer can automatically print a report advising the management of this fact.

Only very large stores can afford point-of-sales terminals at the moment, but many chain stores can take advantage of using bar codes. Local supermarket branches often have labels on the shelves giving the code for the items stored on them. At a certain time of day an assistant will take a bar code decoder for a walk around the store. These devices are available in a variety of shapes and forms and may be as big as a supermarket trolley or as small as a portable tape recorder. A probe shaped like a pen is attached to the device by a wire and as the end of the pen is passed over the bar code labels it reads them. The machine can perform a check to ensure that it has read the code properly and it then stores codes on magnetic tape. The assistant uses the decoder to record any items that are almost out of stock. The tape can then be sent to a computer centre where it is read and used to produce order information for the management.

Exercise 13

1 Make a collection of bar codes from as many different items as possible. Make a note of what the code refers to if this is not obvious.
2 If supermarkets use point of sales terminals for all goods how will they deal with fresh fruit and vegetables? Perhaps they will grow bar coded lettuce!
3 Some libraries are starting to use bar coded library tickets which allow information about the borrower to be entered into a central computer. Visit a local library and find out as much about this system as possible. (If your library has not got such a system ask why not?)

The second data capture system, that used by the boutique, is used by a large number of chain stores. Whenever goods are ordered from a central warehouse and delivered to branches, price tags are attached. These price tags are in two parts, each containing the same data.

The price tickets are called **Kimball tags** (see below) and the information on them is printed in human readable form and coded as a series of punched

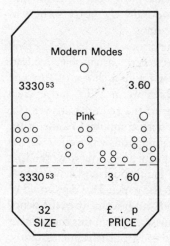

A Kimball price tag

holes. In the boutique the tag would contain a style code, and codes for the colour, size and price of each garment. Half of this tag is left on the item when it is sold. This may be used as a sales receipt. The other half is sent to a computer centre where the tags are put through a Kimball tag reader which transfers the coded data to a computer program.

The computer can use the data from the Kimball tags in several ways. All of the tags from a particular branch can be used to see how many of each item have been sold and from this an order can be produced to replenish that shop's stock. A more usual system is for the computer to collect data from all of its branches and then produce reports to show which branches are selling the most, or which items are the most popular and in which size or colour. From this information the managers can decide on how much stock to order and the colours and sizes that are going to sell the most.

Exercise 14

1 Make a list of all of the stores in your area that use Kimball tags.
2 Write down a list of data items recorded on Kimball tags.
3 Many of the clothes made by Fashion 85 are sold to chains of clothes shops and these stores use the tag method of data capture. Explain how this might be of benefit to Fashion 85, even though they do not sell directly to the public.

Data capture and exams

One day the talk in the Fashion 85 office turned to examinations. The head of department, Frank Stamper, had been giving up some of his spare time to go to night class and study 'O' level chemistry. He had always been interested in science but had never had the opportunity to do any chemistry so he was taking the chance now that he had some spare time.

The main talking point was the way examinations had changed. Frank explained that one of the papers he would have to do was an objective test. Apparently that meant a series of questions, each with a choice of answers. Instead of writing down the answers a special form was provided and a pencil mark could be placed in a box corresponding to the required answer (see opposite). It was, no doubt, something to do with computers. Some of the younger members of staff had done similar examinations when they were at school. Polly said that one of her teachers had explained how it worked.

The completed examination papers could be fed through a machine which could detect the position of the pencil marks on the paper. This data could be fed into a computer and the program could work out how many of the pencil marks agreed with the position of the correct answers. From this the number of marks for the paper could be calculated and a list of the results could be produced. Frank said that he thought that these exams were far easier than

The Northern Exam. Board

Subject

Surname

Forenames

DO NOT FOLD THIS SHEET

Use only an HB pencil

TO CANCEL A MARK
SHADE LOWER PORTION

MARK REQUIRED ANSWER
BY SHADING IN PANEL THUS

Centre No.	Candidate's No.	Subject No.
		0 5 2

Objective test exam paper

the ones he had to take. The girls laughed and said that perhaps he ought to wait until he got his results before saying something like that; he might be in for a shock.

The method of using a computer to read the position of pencil marks on a card or sheet of paper described by Frank is called **mark sensing**. It can be used in many applications where the data required is limited to a small number of choices. The pencil mark can indicate which choice is required. This is ideal for this type of examination where the computer program can decide not only how many questions each candidate got right but can also keep a check on which questions everybody got wrong. The people who set the questions can use this type of information to find out whether the questions were poor or whether candidates were not properly prepared for the exam.

Data capture and banking

Justine Thyme was sitting in a coffee bar in town one day when who should walk in but Jenny Cashpenny, an old friend from school. Over a coffee they started to bring each other up to date on all the gossip—it had been a long time since they had seen each other.

Jenny had got a job in a bank and was very interested to hear about the course that Justine was doing at the college of further education. She knew all about data processing as it was part of her job. Banks today spend a lot of time and effort moving data relating to one bank account to another bank account. Only a small proportion of the bank's business involves moving real money. Justine did not quite understand this so she asked Jenny for more information. 'Well, look at the number of cheques which are used now,' said Jenny. She went on to explain that the cheque is a method of recording data.

'Supposing I owe you some money. I take out my cheque book and write some data on it—the date, amount and your name. Then I sign it and give it to you. When you take it to your bank they will exchange the cheque for cash. What happens is that my cheque has some extra data printed along the bottom in peculiar characters. These give the cheque number, a number identifying the bank at which the account is held and the account number. When the bank receives the cheque some extra data is printed in the same special characters. One of my jobs is to operate the magnetic ink typewriter, and what I would do is type on the cheque the amount of money involved.

'Machines can't read handwriting but they can read these special characters. All of the cheques are then sent off to the computer centre. A special machine is used which magnetises the ink and then reads the magnetic patterns. This machine can transfer all of the magnetic ink data from the cheque to a reel of magnetic tape. The magnetic tape can then be read by a computer. The computer program can then deduct the amount from my bank account and

| Cheque stub | Cheque number | Sorting code | Account number |

SPECIMEN ONLY Issued by Bank Education Service.

_____ 19 __

_____ 19__   00-00-00

BANK OF EDUCATION
HOMETOWN

Pay_____or Order

£_____

000651

⑈000651⑈ 00⑈0000⑆ ⑆047637 5⑈ 30

Sample cheque

add it to yours. This means that I have paid you some money but all that would have changed in the bank is the data.'

Justine and Jenny arranged to meet each other again soon and then Justine had to leave to go and meet her boyfriend. On her way to the meeting she thought a little more about what Jenny had said. She had not given an awful lot of thought to what actually happened in banks, but she now realised that a lot of the work was really data processing. This explained why so many machines were now being used.

Exercise 15

1   Find out what the following are:

a MICR
b OCR

2   Why do the characters on a cheque need to be a special shape and size?
3   Why is the amount written on a cheque in figures and in letters?
4   Visit a bank (or find out by some other means) and discover:

a What is the difference between crossed cheques and open cheques?
b Under what circumstances can you cash a cheque and obtain the money directly and when do you have to wait for a cheque to be 'cleared'?

5   What do you think is meant by clearing a cheque?

Assignment 7

1   A friend of yours works in the local branch of Westfare supermarkets. One day she asks you if you will do her a favour. Apparently, her sister is

Westfare Ltd

Week no 4 4		Branch no		Thousands ‹1› ~2~ ‹4› ‹8›		Hundreds ~1~ ~2~ ‹4› ‹8›	
				Tens ~1~ ‹2› ~4~ ‹8›		Units ‹1› ~2~ ‹4› ‹8›	

Description	Unit	Product code	Qty								
Toothpaste Ultrabrite	48	6006	35	[10]	[20]	[40]	[80]	[1]	[2]	[4]	[8]
Toilet Paper Andrex	24	6017		[10]	[20]	[40]	[80]	[1]	[2]	[4]	[8]
Brillo Pads	12	6028		[10]	[20]	[40]	[80]	[1]	[2]	[4]	[8]
Sugar Silver Spoon	48	6039		[10]	[20]	[40]	[80]	[1]	[2]	[4]	[8]
Washing-up Liquid Fairy	36	604X		[10]	[20]	[40]	[80]	[1]	[2]	[4]	[8]
Cornflakes Kelloggs	24	6050		[10]	[20]	[40]	[80]	[1]	[2]	[4]	[8]
Dog Food Frolic	24	6061		[10]	[20]	[40]	[80]	[1]	[2]	[4]	[8]
Ice Lollies Mr Men	24	6072		[10]	[20]	[40]	[80]	[1]	[2]	[4]	[8]
Fish Fingers Birds Eye	36	6083		[10]	[20]	[40]	[80]	[1]	[2]	[4]	[8]
Frozen Peas Findus	48	6094		[10]	[20]	[40]	[80]	[1]	[2]	[4]	[8]
Pork Sausages Walls	48	6105		[10]	[20]	[40]	[80]	[1]	[2]	[4]	[8]
Orange Squash Kia Ora	24	6116		[10]	[20]	[40]	[80]	[1]	[2]	[4]	[8]
7 UP	12	6127		[10]	[20]	[40]	[80]	[1]	[2]	[4]	[8]
Yorkie Chocolate	48	6138		[10]	[20]	[40]	[80]	[1]	[2]	[4]	[8]
Crisps Tudor	48	6149		[10]	[20]	[40]	[80]	[1]	[2]	[4]	[8]
Digestives McVities	36	615X		[10]	[20]	[40]	[80]	[1]	[2]	[4]	[8]
Crackers Jacobs	48	6160		[10]	[20]	[40]	[80]	[1]	[2]	[4]	[8]
Libby's Orange 'C'	24	6171		[10]	[20]	[40]	[80]	[1]	[2]	[4]	[8]
Lucozade	12	6182		[10]	[20]	[40]	[80]	[1]	[2]	[4]	[8]
Crisp Bread Ryvita	24	6193		[10]	[20]	[40]	[80]	[1]	[2]	[4]	[8]
Marmalade Chivers	36	6204		[10]	[20]	[40]	[80]	[1]	[2]	[4]	[8]
Honey Gales	36	6215		[10]	[20]	[40]	[80]	[1]	[2]	[4]	[8]
Cheese English Cheddar	12	6226		[10]	[20]	[40]	[80]	[1]	[2]	[4]	[8]
Long Life Milk AFF	24	6237		[10]	[20]	[40]	[80]	[1]	[2]	[4]	[8]
Eggs Goldenlay (6)	12	6248		[10]	[20]	[40]	[80]	[1]	[2]	[4]	[8]
Teabags Tetley	12	6259		[10]	[20]	[40]	[80]	[1]	[2]	[4]	[8]
Coffee Powder Nescafe	24	6260		[10]	[20]	[40]	[80]	[1]	[2]	[4]	[8]
S R Flour Be-Ro	24	6271		[10]	[20]	[40]	[80]	[1]	[2]	[4]	[8]
Plain Flour Be-Ro	24	6282		[10]	[20]	[40]	[80]	[1]	[2]	[4]	[8]
Savoury Rice Batchelors	48	6293		[10]	[20]	[40]	[80]	[1]	[2]	[4]	[8]
Raisins Whitworths	36	6304		[10]	[20]	[40]	[80]	[1]	[2]	[4]	[8]
Mustard Colemans English	48	6315		[10]	[20]	[40]	[80]	[1]	[2]	[4]	[8]
Stuffing Mix Paxo	36	6326		[10]	[20]	[40]	[80]	[1]	[2]	[4]	[8]
Chicken Shippams Chunk	24	6337		[10]	[20]	[40]	[80]	[1]	[2]	[4]	[8]
Carrots Smedley sliced	24	6348		[10]	[20]	[40]	[80]	[1]	[2]	[4]	[8]

Supermarket stock order form

getting married on Saturday and they are desperately short staffed at the supermarket. The supervisor said that she could have the day off but it would be extremely helpful if she could get someone to work in her place. You agree to help and when you arrive you find that one of the jobs that the supervisor would like you to help with is the ordering of new stock. This involves walking around the supermarket and looking at the stock on the shelves. The supervisor, Carol Shout (known to the girls as Cashout), accompanies you to show you exactly what to do and she explains the system.

All of the items except fresh fruit and vegetables come from a central warehouse. At the beginning of each month the warehouse sends a catalogue of its stock to the branches. This list is produced in a special way so that if you require any of the items listed all you have to do is mark the quantity with a pencil by putting a line through the appropriate boxes. At the end of the day the completed sheets of the catalogue are returned to the head office. There the separate pages of the book are fed through a machine which 'reads' the marks on the paper and feeds the data to a computer program. This program does several things but the main one is to print out a list of the order on a printer in the warehouse. The staff there can then collect all the items together and put them on a van to be delivered to the branch that ordered them. Having explained this Carol leaves you to get on with the ordering.

a Complete the order form on page 70 to enable the following goods to be ordered. (The first entry for 35 cases of Ultrabrite Toothpaste has been filled in for you.)

- 45 cases of Andrex toilet paper
- 100 cases of Brillo pads
- 50 cases of Silver Spoon sugar
- 60 cases of Kelloggs corn flakes
- 38 boxes of fish fingers
- 50 cases of 7 UP
- 24 cases of Lucozade
- 16 packs of English Cheddar Cheese
- 40 packs of Tetley teabags
- 5 packs of Paxo stuffing mix

b Write the branch code in figures in the box marked *Branch no.* (this is given by the values in the top right-hand side boxes).
c Why are the values written in figures as well as marked in the boxes?
d Why are some items not being ordered?
e How could the week number be recorded so that that too could be read by machine?
f How could the items on the list be written in a different order to make it easier to complete?

2 The Westpool College of Further Education has recently made a

microcomputer available to its students. You have persuaded some trainee programmers to produce a more efficient method of running the dating system (Assignment 4) that proved so popular during charity week (you never know when something like that is going to come in handy). They have agreed to write the programs and you have to provide the data in a form suitable for typing into the computer. Several problems have to be overcome.

Firstly the computer has no key to represent a tick. It was decided that instead of ticks and blanks the data should be represented as a '1' for a tick and a '0' for a blank.

The second problem is that the computer system will only be interested in names and answers to the questions. All of the data from the original forms filled in by the applicants will need to be transferred to a document which will make it easy to type in names and answers to the questions.

Finally, because of the amount of data, some checks have to be built into the system to make sure that errors do not occur. Several checks have been decided on but first of all the forms that were completed for the Westpool College of Further Education Dating Service must be found. Two groups of forms were originally used. These were called F1 and M1.

All of the data must be transferred to input documents (from which data will be typed into the computer), keeping all the boys' data together and all of the girls' data together. This means that two forms are required, M2 and F2.

It has also been decided that because the data will consist of a string of characters consisting only of zeros and ones some check must be made to ensure that the correct data is typed in. After much discussion the following layout was decided on for M2 and F2:

The left-hand column contains the names of all the boys in the batch (more than one form may be required). The centre columns give the items on the original form. Item one in this system was the height. The columns relate to the choices which were available within each item. Finally the hash total is obtained by adding together all of the data items along the row. This can be used to check that the correct data has been entered.

F2 will be similar except for an 'F2' in the corner.

You have the following jobs to do.

a Design and produce batch control forms to make sure that none of the M1 and F1 documents are mislaid.
b Fill in the batch control forms for your own documents.
c Design and produce data entry forms M2 and F2. Remember you are to use your own data items from M1 and F1.

Form no .... of ....

NAME	DATA ITEMS							HASH TOTAL
	1 abcd	2 abcd	3 abcd	4 abcd	5 abcd	6 abcd	7 abcd	
Smith F	0100	0100	1000	0001	0010	1000	1000	7
Fancy J	1000	1000	1000	1010	1100	1000	1000	9

Dating form

6 The development of data processing equipment

From the early days until the 20th century

When data processing was invented by our caveman friends Ug and Og the only equipment required was a sharp stone and a stick. The piece of wood could be called the recording medium since the notches were recorded on it to make a tally stick. The sharpened stone, used to cut the notches, was the first data processing equipment.

Since that time, as the amount of data processing increased so the implements used for the task increased. A great deal of our knowledge of early civilisations comes from the recording of data within them. The early Egyptians used paper made from rushes and the Babylonians used clay tablets. Devices had to be invented and used to record information on these media.

Over the years the increase in manufacturing industry and the growth of trade gave rise to a greater need both for data processing and the means to carry it out. In Asia the abacus developed into the familiar bead frame. Merchants and tradesmen carried these devices from country to country across the civilised world, and many variations of the simple bead frame were invented. These were the first mechanical calculating devices used in data processing. In this country they have rarely found favour, beyond helping young children to count, but in the Far East they are still used as a serious and very efficient calculating aids.

The opening of the trade routes in the seventeenth century brought new methods of calculating. From the Persian Gulf had come a number system consisting of the ten symbols 0 1 2 3 4 5 6 7 8 9. This made life easier for the clerks in Europe to record their daily transactions.

Most commercial data processing at this time consisted of posting accounts which involved writing the details in a ledger with a quill pen. Banking and insurance, as we know them, were in their infancy and commercial data processing requirements were limited as there was only a relatively small quantity of data to process. There were certain areas which did require large volumes of raw data to be processed, but these generally required large numbers of fairly simple calculations to be carried out over and over again on different sets of values (typical of today's data processing applications).

One such area was that of taxation. In France a young mathematician Blaise Pascal realised that his father, a tax inspector, was spending a lot of time on these tax calculations and decided to help by inventing the first mechanical adding machine. This paved the way for true data processing machines. These were generally improved designs of adding machines and mechanical calculating devices which were used, amongst other things, for producing better navigation tables, which in turn allowed a further growth in trade and commerce.

The industrial revolution was marked by an increase in the number of manufacturing industries which required data recording and processing systems to ensure their efficiency. This processing was largely carried out by clerks with nothing more sophisticated than simple mechanical calculators.

To find the next major contribution to the job of the clerk we have to look to America and to one of the largest data processing exercises ever carried out. At the end of the 19th century people were flocking to America from all over the world. The Wild West was opening up and land was being given away to people willing to farm it. News of the gold rushes filtered through to Europe and persuaded people that America was the land of opportunity and they travelled in their thousands, convinced that fortunes were waiting for them. To the American Government this inrush of people caused great problems. A census was carried out every 10 years but because of the increased numbers of people involved it was obvious that the 1887 census would take 13 years to complete.

The answer to the problem came from a young man, himself an immigrant, who adapted an idea originally used in automatic weaving looms. This idea was to transfer the data from the census forms to large punched cards. Herman Hollerith invented one machine to punch the cards, one to sort them and one to list the contents of the cards in a table. This development was to lead the way to automatic data processing systems.

Once the 20th century arrived development of machines to aid data processing increased rapidly. Mechanical calculators became more sophisticated; some of them even had electric motors, allowing them to carry out multiplication and division at the press of a button. Printers were incorporated to show all the calculations that had been carried out and give a permanent record. These electromechanical devices, called **add-listing machines**, were manufactured and used in their thousands up until the late 1960s. Other developments in electromechanical devices could be grouped under the heading of **accounting machines**. These machines were rather like large typewriters. Items could be entered, and the machine would then type the items in the correct columns on ledger cards. By pressing the appropriate keys arithmetic operations could be carried out and the results would be printed on the cards. Some of these machines are still in use but they are gradually being replaced by other devices.

Scientific and commercial data processing

The term data processing as we have used it refers to **commercial data processing** within an organisation. However, there is another kind of data processing. Scientists, engineers and mathematicians all have to convert various specialist forms of data, obtained from experiments, to useful information. This usually involves carrying out a lot of fairly complicated mathematics on a fairly small amount of data. These calculations used to be worked out using the sort of calculating devices available to the commercial data processor. However, in the early 1940s this changed. The changes (partly as a result of research financed by governments who were trying to win the war) were brought about by the invention of the computer.

These early computers were very large, extremely unreliable, required a large amount of power to run them and cost a lot to build. Compared to the devices they replaced, though, they represented such an enormous increase in power that one leading scientist said that four computers would be able to carry out all the calculating requirements of the world.

It did not take very long for commercial interests to realise that if these new-fangled computers could do complex arithmetic quickly for scientists then they should also be able to carry out relatively simple business calculations even more quickly. In 1948 representatives of Lyons, the tea and coffee company, approached the electronics company Ferranti to look at the possibility of building a commercial computer to carry out wage calculations. A machine was built and given the name LEO (Lyons Electronic Office). When it started on Christmas Eve 1951 it represented a major step forward. Wages calculations were performed in two-and-a-half minutes instead of the eight minutes they took manually.

A new industry grew up supplying computer equipment for commercial data processing applications, but up until the early 1970s these machines were very expensive and it was only the larger firms that could afford them.

Gradually, with improvements in manufacturing techniques and new developments in electronic components (the invention of the **transistor**, for example), the size and price of computers came down while at the same time they were able to process more and more data. They became more versatile and more widespread. The invention of the **integrated circuit**, which is commonly known as the **silicon chip**, allowed the computer to become very cheap, very powerful, and hence very common, even in fairly small businesses.

The integrated circuit is a method of squeezing lots of electronic components into a very small space in a wafer of silicon. Perhaps 20 000 components may be contained in a package half a centimetre square. What is more, silicon chips are cheap to produce.

In data processing the first machine to be affected by this new development was the calculator. The old mechanical and electromechanical devices were expensive to produce, but the new all-electronic calculators became cheaper, almost by the day. Electronic calculators were extremely fast and accurate and had no moving parts to wear out. Today the electronic calculator is an extremely common device, almost taken for granted in the office, whereas its mechanical counterpart has all but disappeared.

The silicon chip gave birth to the microcomputer which in many cases is very much more powerful than LEO and yet may be only slightly larger than a typewriter. These machines have replaced accounting machines and add listers in the modern office.

Exercise 16

1 What do the following initials stand for?

a IBM
b ICL
c NCR

What is the importance of these companies to data processing?
2 Draw a time chart to show the development of data processing equipment, starting with the tally stick and going through to the modern computer.

Today's computer is certainly not the final development in data processing, nor is it the only technological change to take place. Devices are continually becoming more powerful while at the same time decreasing in size and price. For example, the typewriter has developed into the **word processor**, factory production is carried out by computerised robot machines, and major advances in applying lasers to data transmission equipment mean that work patterns are being changed. These changes mean that the Fashion 85 office of the future may be a very different place to the office of today.

7 Calculators

The electronic calculator and the computer are the main data processing tools in modern businesses. We have seen how the development of these devices has caused the price to fall and size to decrease while the power has increased. They are now available in several standard shapes and sizes.

The features of a calculator

Many parents are now heard to exclaim in horror at examination time that 'things aren't what they used to be'. In their day they had to learn sums, they all knew their tables and didn't need fancy machines to do their arithmetic for them. 'Not like today—you can actually take calculators into examination rooms!'

What they do not realise of course is that the calculator is a marvellous device but it is still at the mercy of the operator. Arithmetic can certainly be carried out extremely quickly and accurately, but what that arithmetic is depends on the skill of the person using the calculator. This means that as far as teaching arithmetic is concerned the emphasis has changed: our parents carried out repetitive sums in order to obtain accuracy in the use of numbers and figures; we can now concentrate on learning different methods for working out problems, leaving the calculator to handle the boring repetitive problems.

Calculators differ slightly in modes of operation and in the facilities they offer, and learning how to use these different facilities is extremely important. Many very cheap calculators will do no more than add, subtract, multiply and divide. At the other end of the scale there are devices costing hundreds of pounds which are very close to being powerful computers. All calculators have four main components.

Keyboard

This facility allows calculations to be typed in. In cheap calculators this may consist of a set of buttons for the digits (0–9) and buttons for the arithmetic operators (+, −, ×, ÷, =). This is called a **numeric keypad**.

On more sophisticated devices the individual keys may carry out several independent operations and the sequence of key depressions required for any given operation has to be found initially from the operating instructions.

Many keyboards have a bleep facility. This emits a high-pitched sound when a key is depressed and acts as a signal to the operator to say that that number or operation has been accepted by the machine. This means that the operator does not have to look at the display as she presses each key and is an aid to avoiding mis-keying. Another feature of some calculators is a touch-sensitive keyboard which responds to the tips of the fingers without the need for pressing buttons.

Display

The display is the window which allows the operator to see the numbers as they are input. It also displays the results of any arithmetic.

Two types of display are commonly used on calculators. The **liquid crystal** type gives black characters on a silver display and has the great advantage of requiring very little power to run it. Coloured displays, produced by devices called *light emitting diodes* (LEDs), are generally easier to see and are available with choices of red, green or blue numbers on a black background, but these require a fairly large amount of electricity to maintain the display. This is sometimes important if batteries are used.

Power supply

Some method of providing the electricity to drive the machine is obviously needed. In most cases this power requirement is very small, which means that **batteries** can be used. This makes calculators very portable, whereas old-fashioned electromechanical devices had to be plugged into the mains.

Batteries, however, do run out, usually at the most inconvenient times, so manufacturers often supply a **transformer**. This allows electronic calculators to be run from the mains, thus giving a choice of mains or battery power.

Another development which is being incorporated into many machines is the use of **solar power**. A set of windows on the top of the machine collects light (daylight or light from electric lights). The circuitry inside the machine can use this light to recharge special batteries during use. This makes the batteries last a long time and, if they do still happen to run down, the calculator can often be plugged into the mains to be recharged. These calculators do tend to be expensive.

Electronic circuitry

Inside the case are the components that make a calculator work. It is the circuitry which governs whether the calculator is simple or sophisticated. These workings may make the calculator small enough to fit into a wrist-watch. Alternatively, when it is not being used for calculations, they may allow it to tell the time, the date, or even remind the operator of business meetings, birthdays and wedding anniversaries.

Calculators are available with many features and facilities, some of which are helpful and some of which are expensive luxuries. Three common ones are memory, percent and constant. One or more memories may be available, allowing the operator to store parts of calculations. For example, let us work out the length of a fence around a rectangular garden 10.362 metres long by 8.513 metres wide. One way of doing it might be to put in 10.362 and multiply it by 2. Store this answer in the memory. Then key in 8.513 and multiply by 2. Then add the number stored in the memory to obtain the final answer. This avoids the need to write down the results of intermediate calculations and so makes the operation quicker.

Printer calculators

It is often very important to keep a written record of the calculations that have been carried out. This record helps to guide another person through the calculations and provides a reference copy which can be checked if an error is thought to have occurred. Many modern desk-top and some pocket calculators have a small printer built in which records the calculations, usually on a roll of paper two inches wide.

Scientific and programmable calculators

Despite the fact that the price of calculators has dropped over the last few years, almost to the point where they give away the calculator when you pay for the box it is packed in, it is still possible to buy expensive calculators. These are usually called **scientific** calculators because they have special keys which enable the operator to work out complicated mathematical formulae and expressions. Many of these devices are specialist tools for specific use, eg statistics, engineering.

Another type of calculator which is becoming increasingly common is the **programmable** type. This allows the operator to type in a number of steps required in a calculation and store them, just as a computer stores a computer program. The calculations can then be carried out over and over again using different numbers. For example, if you wanted to work out the volumes of lots of different-sized boxes you might have a program that says:

- key in number
- store number in memory
- key in number
- multiply by the number in memory
- store in memory

- key in number
- multiply by the number in memory.

Each of these instructions would be input by pressing specific keys on the keyboard. Another key would be available, called the RUN key. When this key is pressed the first three numbers—the length, breadth and height of the first box—could be entered and the calculator would automatically run through the set of instructions and display the volume of the box. The RUN key could then be pressed again, the numbers for the second box entered and it would automatically work out the volume of that. This process could be repeated as many times as required. When all of the calculations are complete the program could be changed so that the machine could work through another sequence of instructions. The best and most expensive of these machines will even store the sequence of instructions (the **program**) when it is switched off. All calculators of this type are, however, quite complicated to use.

Exercise 17

1 Use a calculator to work out answers to the following questions.
Remember: the order in which you carry out the operations is important.
Anything inside brackets must be done before other calculations. Multiplication or division must be done before addition or subtraction.

a 3.1876 + 7.9213 − 10.001
b 3.643 + 5 × 3.187
c (3.643 + 5) × 3.187
d 6.487 × 2.136 + 18.63
e 6.487 × (2.136 + 18.63)
f 6.487 − 2.136 + 18.63

g 6.487 − (2.136 + 18.63)
h 2.538 × 99.62 − 4.38
i 5.162 + 18.637 − 4.923 × 6.15
j 5.162 + 18.637 − (4.923 × 6.15)
k 265.7 − 9.6 + 100.035
l 265.7 − (9.6 + 100.035)

2 Calculate the following amounts. If your calculator has a percent key it may help you with the questions. (You will have to look in the instruction book to find out how to use it.)

a 5.60 + 3% of 5.60
b 124.35 − 10% of 124.35
c 17% of 24.60

d 12.5% of 16.83
e 125% of 99.86
f 0.5% of 3126.30

3 The following calculations will require several stages. The answers to each stage will have to be written down. (If your calculator has a memory you may find that you can use that instead.)

a (3.15 + 9.26) × (13.7 − 6.5)
b (95.837 − 22.62) − (17.32 + 8.654)
c (22.93 − 6.41) × (18.93 + 2.63) − (2.9 + 6.2)
d 13.4 + 9.6 × (18.6 + 3.2) − (2.1 + 3.2)
e 6.3 × (6.3 − 3.1) × (6.3 − 4.2) × (6.3 − 5.3)
f 2 × (3.42 + 8.431) × (3.42 + 6.431)

Warning: just because a calculator has been used does not mean that the answer is right. Ask yourself, 'Is this a reasonable answer?' If it is not CHECK your arithmetic.

Assignment 8

In the Fashion 85 office calculators are used so much that they are taken for granted. The only time that they are examined in any detail (except on the rare occasion when one breaks down) is when some new device comes on the market and the existing ones are due to be renewed.

Somebody in the office recently said that *all* calculators have some hidden functions which are rarely used. You have decided to see if this is true so you try some experiments with your calculator.

1   Press the following keys and write down the answers you obtain:

a $2 \times =$ d $5 \times =$
b $3 \times =$ e $16 \times =$
c $4 \times =$

2   Repeat this with the following key sequences. *Do not press CLEAR between questions.*

a $5 + 3 =$ d $7 =$
b $3 =$ e $3.71 =$
c $2 =$

3   Explain what the two functions in questions 1 and 2 are. Can you find any other hidden functions? Try pressing $2 - =$ and see what happens.
4   What happens when overflow (a number becomes too big for the display) or a divide by 0 error occurs? Try multiplying the following numbers: $877379999 \times 777499998$. Try dividing 835175 by 0.
5   It was your birthday recently and your maiden aunt in Grimsby sent you £20. As your calculator has seen better days you decide that it might be a good idea to replace it but there are so many different types on the market that you find it difficult to decide which one to buy. You need the calculator for the work you are doing at college.

Visit some shops that deal in calculators and look at office equipment catalogues. Decide which calculator you would like to buy and then write down the following details about it.

a Name.
b Type (simple, scientific, programmable, printer, etc).
c Colour of display.
d Type of display (LED, liquid crystal, etc).

e Number of digits in display.
f Type of power supply. If batteries say how many and what type.
g Functions available (+, −, ×, ÷, etc). List as many of these functions as possible.
h Price.
i Name of retailer.

8 Computers

What is a computer?

Computers are problem-solving tools which are capable of operating at extremely high speed.

Whenever a problem has to be solved a certain procedure has to be followed. This can be shown by the following chart:

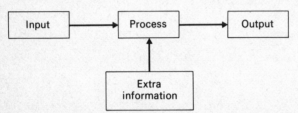

Suppose you want to answer a question in an exercise in this book. First you read the question. This is the *input* stage and your eyes can be called the *input device*. You then *process* the data to find the answer to the question and then you write down the answer. This is the *output* stage and the pen and paper are the *output device*.

At the process stage the data you work on may be in your brain and the processing involved may be merely to organise your thoughts. Sometimes you will have to get data from elsewhere. You may visit the library and get extra data relating to the question. This must be sifted through to provide the information required to answer the question. Nearly all problem solving can be broken down into these stages.

Exercise 18

Fill in the operations to be carried out under the appropriate headings for the following tasks in the table.

Task	Input	Process	Output	Extra information
a Bake a cake				
b Make a telephone call				
c Answer these questions				
d Find a chapter in this book				
e Enrol for a course at college				

What does a computer consist of?

When computers were invented it seemed logical to build units or pieces of equipment into them to carry out the tasks which humans had to do to solve problems. This means that the computer is not a single machine but a collection of machines. The number of actual devices included varies with the size of the computer. All computers tend to have the same types of devices:

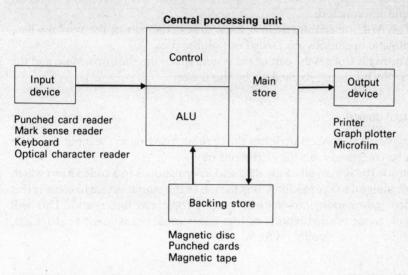

The constituent parts of a computer

Input device

This is the general term given to any machine which passes data to the central processor. This can be compared with the office in tray which allows work to be input for processing.

In a computerised system a device has to translate from some form understandable to people to a form which the computer can understand. We have already seen some methods of coding information in this way—punched cards, bar codes, mark sensing. Each of these can be read by machines which pass the data to the central processor.

Central processing unit

This is the machine which is usually called 'the computer'. It is usually referred to as the CPU. This is the part of the system which carries out most of the work. It can be compared with the clerk or typist in the office, carrying out tasks on data under the direction of her supervisor.

Sets of instructions, called **programs**, are stored in the CPU. These instructions tell the system how the data is to be treated—which operations have to be carried out. The parts of the CPU have special functions and these are reflected in the names of the parts.

The **control unit** is responsible for making sure that the instructions are carried out in the correct order. Signals sent from this unit can wake up the input device and say that processing cannot continue until more data is supplied or they can tell the output device that the processor is ready to output information.

The ALU or **arithmetic and logic unit** is the part of the system where arithmetic operations are carried out on the data.

The **main store** is the part of the system that holds the instructions and the data which is being worked on by the system.

Output device

This part of the system performs the opposite function to the input device. It can be compared with the clerk's out tray.

Inside the system all of the data and information is in a coded form which is meaningful to the machine. It is the job of the output device to convert this coded information into a form which people can understand. This will usually mean printed reports or lists but it could equally well be diagrams, graphs, or even directly on to microfilm.

Backing store

This is used, like the office filing cabinets, to store the information which may not be required at the present time but which will be required in the future. This data in the computer system is stored in a form which the machine can easily read—on magnetic tape or magnetic disc.

Exercise 19

1   Here is a list of computer devices. Rewrite the names under the appropriate heading—*input*, *output* or *backing store*.

a punched card reader
b line printer
c magnetic tape unit
d graph plotter
e magnetic disc unit
f paper tape reader

2   Write the headings *input*, *output*, *storage* and *input/output*. Find the names of as many different computer devices as possible and write them under the appropriate headings.

Computer languages

A large number of languages are used by computers. They each have their own special features which make them suitable for certain applications.

Machine code

The actual language in which the machine operates. This is basically a set of coded instructions which is different for each type of computer. It is quite difficult to write programs in this language as it requires a good knowledge of the machinery. Generally programs are written in another language and a program is used to translate to machine code.

Assembler and Plan

These are called **low-level languages**. They are very close to machine code. A program called an **assembler** translates low-level language programs to machine code before they can be run.

High-level languages

Languages designed to be close to that in which the programmer would normally solve a problem. Mathematical languages use lots of symbols, while commercial languages use sentences. A program called a **compiler** translates high-level language programs to machine code.

COBOL

The most common high-level commercial language. Designed to handle large files of data easily with instructions very like written English.

FORTRAN

FORmula TRANslator—a scientific language written as a series of mathematical formulae.

PL1

Programming Language 1—a general-purpose language designed for commercial and scientific use.

RPG

Report Program Generator—a system designed to carry out simple operations on files without the need to learn the more complicated languages.

ALGOL

ALGOrithmic Language—for mathematical and scientific applications.

Among the other languages available are PASCAL, PILOT, COMAL and BASIC.

Hardware and software

The machines and devices which make up a computer system are called the **hardware** (computer people say that this means anything that you can trip over in a computer room!). Before a computer can do anything useful two other parts are needed.

The first of these is **software** which is a general term given to all of the *programs* required by and run on the computer.

A program is a set of instructions, written in a language which the computer understands, which allows it to carry out a task.

There are two types of software, commonly called **systems software** and **applications software** (or applications packages). The first refers to the programs required by the computer system to allow it to work. They are usually supplied with the computer and they enable the operators to communicate with the system. The second type of program—an applications software program—carries out the tasks required by the user, eg payroll programs work out wages, accounts programs process ledger details. These programs may be written by a programmer working for the company or they may be bought from a company which specialises in writing computer programs (a **software house**).

Before the system can produce useful results the programs require some *data* upon which to operate. The data is converted to a suitable form and is operated on by the computer program which converts it into information.

Mainframes, minis and micros

Computers, like boxes of washing powder, come in three different sizes.

The smallest size are called **microcomputers**. In these most of the tasks of the central processing unit are carried out by a single very powerful silicon chip and the complete system is often housed in one box little bigger than an electric typewriter (see opposite).

The next size up is called the **minicomputer** which usually has the CPU and backing store housed in a cabinet the size of a fridge–freezer. Technically these are far more complex and more powerful than the microcomputer. They usually have a number of different input and output devices attached to them.

The largest computers are called **mainframes**. These are very complex and have many different input and output devices. They also use a number of different backing store devices, which means that the computer system usually requires a room full of machines. These machines often have special operating requirements; it is usually necessary to provide them with air

A microcomputer with typewriter keyboard and visual display screen

conditioning and filtration systems which keep the temperature and humidity constant and get rid of any dust in the air. False floors are usually built into these rooms so that the cables connecting the devices can run out of the way under the floor.

Most computers are capable of doing a large number of jobs at the same time. The larger the computer, the more expensive it is but the more data processing tasks it can do simultaneously. Because of the range of computer equipment available it is possible to match a system to the needs of the company.

Microcomputers are capable of carrying out one or two operations at a time on files where the number of records is measured in hundreds. The size of the main store is measured in **kilobytes**, where *kilo* means 1024 and *byte* means the amount of storage needed for 1 coded character. Hence, a 64K system can store 65 536 characters. In computing terms microcomputers tend to be slow but they are still capable of carrying out operations many thousands of times faster than people.

Minicomputers are faster still and they are capable of doing ten or more jobs at the same time. The main store size is measured in millions of bytes. They have sufficient capacity to be able to do many jobs at the same time on files containing thousands of records.

Mainframes are used by large firms with large files containing hundreds of thousands of records. Many users can be connected to these computers so that perhaps a hundred jobs (at busy times) might be on the go at the same time. As the company grows, extra input, output and backing store devices (called **peripherals**) can be added if extra capacity is needed.

Exercise 20

1 Several companies are thinking of buying computers (or changing their existing machines). What type of machine (micro, mini, mainframe or none) would you expect each company to buy?

a ICI—a very large chemical company employing thousands of people. Millions of customers worldwide buy fertilisers and plastics from this company.

b ISA Controls Ltd—a small engineering company employing 30 people. They have several hundred customers and suppliers.

c Smiths Insurance Brokers—an insurance broker employing about a dozen staff. They deal with several hundred insurance companies and have thousands of customers. They have to keep track of all the policies offered by the insurance companies.

d Joseph Lucas Ltd—manufacturers of electrical components for the motor and aerospace industries. They have several factories and employ many thousands of people.

e Decorative Ironwork—a company producing wrought-iron gates. Recently formed and at present employing 3 people, they have 80 or 90 customers.

f James Graham Ltd—a timber importer dealing with hundreds of customers and suppliers. They employ about 30 staff.

2 Make a note of the type of peripheral devices each company might need.
3 Discuss the types of peripheral device with the rest of your group and check their suggestions against your list.

Fashion 85 microcomputer system

Jean Byers, the head of the Purchasing Department of Fashion 85, has recently bought a microcomputer. For quite a time she had been interested in the possibility of applying a computer to certain functions within the department and as the price dropped she saw the possibility coming closer to reality. Several months ago she visited a computer exhibition and this was followed by visits to showrooms to talk to computer salesmen. Eventually she managed to find a suitable system and a company were willing to provide the programs at a reasonable cost.

When it was eventually delivered, Jean and her assistant, M T Pockett, were given a demonstration by Mr S Chip who had been responsible for writing the programs. He showed them how to switch the processor on and how to load the *floppy discs* that held the programs. The processor automatically read a program from the floppy disc and some information was displayed on the screen attached to the processor. Mr Chip then demonstrated how the typewriter keyboard attached to the processor could be used to enter information or data.

It was explained that the computer could not give answers to just *any* questions but that it had been set up to guide the person using the system through a series of questions and instructions. The computer displayed the questions on the screen and the answers were typed in on the keyboard. When it was switched on the operator could carry out a dialogue with the machine.

Computer	FASHION 85 PURCHSYS ESTIMATING AND SUPPLIERS SYSTEM DO YOU WANT ESTIMATING SYSTEM (E) OR SUPPLIERS FILES (S)?
Jean Byers	S
Computer	DO YOU WANT TO CHANGE SUPPLIERS FILE (C) OR INTERROGATE (I)?
Jean Byers	I
Computer	SUPPLIERS FILE NOT PRESENT—PLEASE LOAD SUPPLIERS FILE AND PRESS 'C' TO CONTINUE OR 'A' TO ABORT
Jean Byers	A
Computer	DO YOU NOW WANT ESTIMATING SYSTEM (E) SUPPLIERS FILES (F) OR EXIT (X)?
Jean Byers	X
Computer	FASHION 85 PURCHSYS END OF RUN

It became obvious that quite a lot of work was going to be involved in using the computer, but Mr Chip assured the ladies that once they had set up the required files, read the operating instructions and got used to the system they would be wondering how they had ever managed without it.

After Mr Chip had left Jean discussed with Myra Pockett what had happened. The system had been purchased to deal with two areas of the department's work.

Firstly, a large part of the job involved estimating. If the department was to supply the Production Department with raw materials then they would have to work out how much of each type of material would be required and this would depend on the particular designs which were to be produced. In the past this had involved a lot of work with calculators to work through the complicated mathematics involved. Jean realised, however, that she was going through the same type of calculation over and over again with different values, depending on the designs she was working on. She realised that if she could get a computer program to carry out these calculations then all she would have to do would be to supply it with the appropriate dimensions and the computer would work out the amount of material required.

The second job the computer was required for was to organise the files of information relating to the suppliers of materials. Jean wanted to be able to ask the computer who could supply a particular type of material; the computer program would examine the files and would then give the name of the company which usually met the requirements.

The system had been bought to carry out these tasks and Mr Chip had assured them that it would do the job. Myra was a little perturbed because the initial demonstration had not been that impressive.

Jean explained to her that the problem was that at the moment the suppliers' files were in the filing cabinets, as they had always been. Before the computer could do its job all the information held on those files would have to be put on to floppy disc. This would mean using that part of the program that normally changes the supplier's file, to type in all of the details to create that file. This data would then be stored on floppy disc by the computer. Until that was done the computer would have no data to process. This part of the program would also be used later to add details of new suppliers to the file or to remove suppliers whom Fashion 85 were no longer dealing with.

It would obviously take some time to get this part of the system working. In the meantime the part of the program which carried out the calculations could be used as soon as they had worked out how to use it and trained some of the other members of the department.

Within a couple of days of obtaining the system Jean approached Frank Stamper and asked if she could 'borrow' a member of staff to type the suppliers' files on to the computer system. Frank suggests that it would be good experience for you, especially as you are studying data processing anyway. By this time Jean has read the manuals and is now familiar with what the system requires.

When you arrive in the Purchasing Department Jean shows you how to switch on the machine, how to insert the program disc and how to insert the data disc. You can then go through the system.

Computer	FASHION 85 PURCHSYS ESTIMATING AND SUPPLIERS SYSTEM DO YOU WANT ESTIMATING (E) OR SUPPLIERS FILES (S)?
U R Keen	S
Computer	DO YOU WANT TO CHANGE (C) OR INTERROGATE (I)?
U R Keen	C

Computer	DO YOU WANT TO INSERT (I), DELETE (D), CREATE (C) OR DESTROY (K)?
U R Keen	C
Computer	FILENAME?
U R Keen	SUP1/MMF
Computer	FILE SUPI/MMF BEING CREATED RECORD NO 1 COMPANY NAME?

Jean has given you copies of the file containing the names and addresses of suppliers of manmade fibres to start on and from this file you obtain the information to put on to the computer records.

U R Keen	ASKRIGG MILLS LTD
Computer	ADDRESS?
U R Keen	ASKRIGG, YORKS
Computer	PRODUCTS SUPPLIED?
U R Keen	T63:T64:C32
Computer	COMMENTS?
U R Keen	DELIVERY WITHIN WEEK

The computer then displays the record on the screen and asks if the information is correct. You type in 'Y' for yes, having first checked the record against the original file copy. The disc drive then clicks and whirrs for a short time as the computer transfers this record to disc. A message on the screen appears asking for the next record and you go through this same procedure for every record on the file.

When you have completed this file it will be possible for anybody in the Purchasing Department to type in a request to interrogate the file. The system will ask what product code is required and when the code is typed in it will read through the file and print out the name and address of every company supplying that product.

The system actually has two separate output devices. The screen is very useful for displaying information quickly but it is not suitable if you want to take the information away, perhaps to send it to somebody else. In this situation a printed copy (**hard copy** or **printout**) is required and for this purpose a printer is attached to the system.

When Jean was buying the system she examined the available printers very carefully. Two main types were available. The first one printed at very high speeds—500 to 800 words per minute—but this produced characters as a series of dot patterns (**dot matrix printer**):

```
                    FASHION 85 PURCHSYS
                    ====================

            ESTIMATING AND SUPPLIERS SYSTEM


DO YOU WANT ESTIMATING SYSTEM (E) OR SUPPLIERS FILES (F) ? F
```

Dot matrix printout

The second type produced print at a lower speed (300–500 wpm) but gave extremely high-quality output. This type is known as a **daisy wheel** printer because the typeface is embossed on the ends of the spokes of a wheel (known as petals). The wheel spins around on the printer and when the character to be printed passes the ribbon a little hammer gives the petal a tap and pushes the print through the ribbon and on to the paper. It was felt that the extra cost of this type of printer was probably worthwhile in view of the high print quality. It also had the advantage of being able to change to different print styles by simply changing the daisy wheel.

Jean explains that to get information printed is simply a matter of typing in a single word command and then making sure that the printer is switched on and loaded with paper. However, should you forget to put paper in then the printer reminds you by emitting a high-pitched buzz.

It is also necessary for Jean to show you how to load the printer. She explains that the printer has two options: single sheet, which means that paper can be put in exactly as with a typewriter; or tractor feed, which means that a continuous roll of paper is fed through the printer (**continuous stationery**). The paper has a row of holes along each side and these must fit over teeth at each side of the printer; clips then make sure that the paper stays in position. The teeth drive the paper through the machine and make sure that it does not slip and this makes sure that the print is correctly aligned on the paper. Loading the paper can be a tricky operation and requires a little practice.

Another task which Jean explains to you is that of copying discs. After spending a lot of time typing in data it would be a serious problem if something happened to the disc (and they do wear out), making it necessary to do the work all over again.

To protect against such a mishap Jean suggests that you use the command which copies discs to make duplicates of all the files. These copies (**backup copies**) could be kept in the safe and only used if something happened to the files which were being used.

Having spent half a day explaining the system to you, Jean then leaves you to finish the job of setting up the files.

Exercise 21

1 List the procedures which Jean Byers has asked you to carry out on the new computer system.

2 A glossary is a list of technical words and their meanings. Computers have a lot of technical terms associated with them. Put a heading *Glossary of computing terms* on a sheet of paper. Divide the paper into two columns, with a left-hand column about one-third the width of the sheet of paper. Read through the passage above and whenever you come across a technical term write that word in the left-hand column and its meaning (in your own words) in the right-hand column. This will give you a sort of computer dictionary. *Keep this up to date throughout the rest of the course.*

3 Find the meaning of the following terms by carrying out some research in the library, then put the words in your glossary.

a Bit
b Byte
c Bi-directional printing.

4 How many different sizes and types of floppy disc are there? Refer to advertisements in computing magazines and write down as many different sizes and types as possible. Be careful that you find different *types* and not just discs made by different manufacturers.

5 A computer program is a sequence of instructions which are to be carried out. Many devices can be programmed—automatic washing machines, central heating systems—which means that they come on at a certain time, perform a sequence of operations and then switch themselves off. It is even possible to write programs for ordinary calculators. For example, press the following sequence of keys on a calculator:

$$5 + 3 = \times 7 =$$

You have followed through a sequence of operations and the answer 56 should have appeared. Write programs in the same way to do the following.

a Work out the area of a square with sides 3 cm long.
b Work out how much pay you have earned if you get £1.56 per hour for a 37.5-hour week.
c One-third of your wages goes to pay tax, national insurance and other deductions. Write a program to work out your take-home pay if your earnings were the same as in *b*.

Fashion 85 Computer Section

To remain competitive, in recent years Fashion 85 has found that an increasing amount of work has to be carried out by computer. The original equipment, bought in 1970, had entailed a massive amount of work and the reorganisation of the Accounts Department. When it became obvious that a computer was required because of the amount of work being carried out several possibilities seemed open to the company.

Two main options were discussed and after a great deal of deliberation it was decided that rather than set up a completely new Computing Department the Accounts Department should be expanded and computing equipment should be sited there. Ed Sorter was appointed as Data Processing Manager and he worked with his boss Tilley Spencer to buy the computer equipment and organise the new staff required to run it. In many cases this staff were people already working for Fashion 85 who were retrained to work as data preparation staff or computer operators.

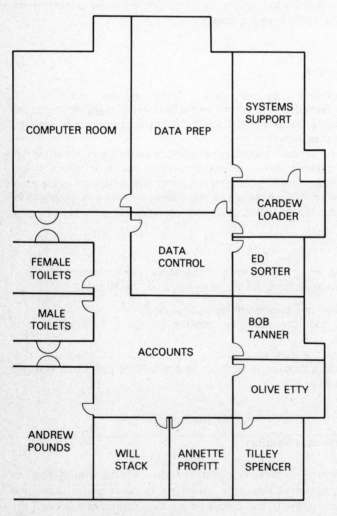

Plan of the Accounts Department offices

Fashion 85 computer room

A lot of work was involved in setting up the initial system to make it useful to the company. Programs had to be written and tested, files had to be transferred from filing cabinets to the computer system. This work originally took almost a year to complete and during that time many people in the company thought that the whole thing had been a mistake.

At the end of that first year a lot of work of the Accounts Department was being carried out by computer. Wages were calculated, taxes and deductions worked out, payslips were printed and reports could be produced to tell the managers of each department how many hours had been worked and the overtime situation. The Wages Section received a cash report which gave details of the number of coins of each denomination required to make up all of the pay packets. This made a lot of difference to the work load of the people involved and they started to see that these computers may have something going for them after all.

Over the years since its installation the number of jobs carried out by the computing section has increased considerably. Nearly every department uses the computer for one reason or another. Changes have been made in the equipment and more and more of the old Accounts Department offices have been taken over and equipped with machines connected with the computer. Production control, stock control, wages, accounting, personnel and transport data is all fed into the computer and programs operate on this data to produce magnetic tape files, magnetic disc files or printed lists and reports of various types.

The Section is now divided into four separate parts, all under the control of Ed Sorter. These are Data Control, Data Preparations, Operations and Systems Support.

Data control

When data is taken for processing it is usually recorded on source documents, ie timesheets, stock record sheets, etc. During the week these are taken to data reception which is part of the Data Control section. The documents are usually in batches and one of the jobs carried out by data control is to work out batch control totals, hash totals and so on. Checks are made to ensure that the correct number of sheets have been delivered and the control values are recorded so that they can be checked against the values the computer produces. These procedures help to detect any errors which may occur while the documents are being processed. Data Control is also responsible for getting the results back to the people using the system and this will entail some other processes.

The output from the computer is usually in the form of sheets of computer printout. The extremely high print speeds mean that the paper has to be fed through the printer as a continuous sheet. The length of paper is divided into page lengths by perforations which make it easy to divide it up into single sheets.

Quite often the paper comes in sets with carbon paper sandwiched between sheets of printout, to enable copies to be produced. The data control clerks have to deal with boxes of this material and to send it back to the user in a suitable form. To do this quickly equipment has been developed to divide the carbon sheets from the printout (**decollators**) and to split it into single sheets (**bursters**). Sometimes **guillotines** have to be used to trim the output and when the clerks have carried out further checks to ensure that all of the data has been processed they return the output to the user.

Data preparation

When Data Control has ensured that the job for processing is complete it is passed to Data Preparation, where the Supervisor distributes the source documents among the operators.

At Fashion 85 they have recently installed the latest system of preparing data for input to a computer. This is called a **key-to-disc** system (see below). Each of the operators sits at a **visual display unit** (VDU) which looks like a television set with a keyboard attached. Any information typed on the keyboard is displayed on the screen. These are connected to a minicomputer and this can send information to the screen. Similarly, the information keyed in can be sent to this computer.

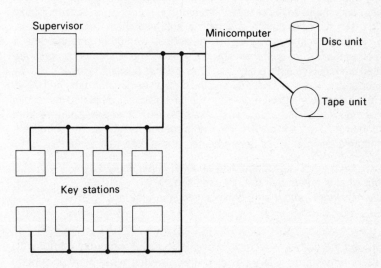

Key-to-disc data preparation system

When the operator is given a job she types in a job number on the keyboard. The computer then displays an image of the source document on the screen. The operator can then copy the values from the original document on to the displayed image. When she has finished she can check to make sure that she has not made any mistakes, then she presses the SEND key on the keyboard.

The data is then passed to the computer, which carries out some more checks (check digit calculations, for example). If the data is accepted it is transferred to a magnetic disc and the next document is displayed on the screen.

When the complete job has been entered the operator passes the source documents to another girl who calls up the job and types in a code number to tell the computer to verify the data. This girl then retypes all of the source documents and the computer checks that the data agrees with that typed by the first girl. If it does not she retypes it.

Every few hours, when a number of jobs have been completed, the supervisor types in an instruction telling the computer to **dump** the contents of the magnetic disc on to a magnetic tape. The computer must then organise the data so that all of the work relating to a particular job stays together on the tape. The reel of magnetic tape containing the data in coded form can then be taken to the operations room to be processed on the main computer system. The supervisor can use her master console to keep track of how jobs are progressing as well as deciding when to carry out the dumps.

Exercise 22

1   Copy out the following passage and fill in the missing words.

The departments of Fashion 85 which use the data processing facilities deliver the source documents to the reception area of the .... section. Clerks check the data to make sure it is complete and also check the .... totals. Records are kept to show the jobs that have been worked on and the data is passed on to the .... section supervisor. The source documents are distributed amongst the girls to be .... and are then passed on to be .... by another operator. The supervisor dumps the data on to magnetic tape and this is passed on to operations to be run. When the job has been completed the results are passed back to .... where the sheets of paper are separated from the carbon by a .... and divided into single sheets by a .... The sheets are finally trimmed using a .... before being passed back to the user.

2   What will happen if Data Control find an error in the data?
3   Find out what is meant by pre-printed stationery.
4   Put any new words and their meanings into your glossary.

Operations

The Computer Operations Section houses the main computer equipment. Fashion 85 now has quite a large mainframe computer with many peripheral devices.

Fashion 85 computer system—technical specification

Mainframe computer

ICL 2904 with 128K word main store. Word length 24 bits.

Peripherals

Card reader—800 cards per minute.
   2 line printers—1600 lines per minute, 160 characters per line.
   6 disc drives—60 megabytes (million characters) per drive, 500 000 characters per second transfer rate.
   4 magnetic tape drives—300 000 characters per second transfer rate.
   64 terminals consisting of 50 VDUs and 14 teletypes. These are connected to various offices throughout the organisation. Those outside Westpool are connected via rented Post Office Datel lines.

Front end processor

Minicomputer used for communications processing. This computer keeps track of data received by the mainframe from remote terminals and ensures that the correct terminal gets the answers.

Data preparation computer

Minicomputer with disc drive and magnetic tape unit. VDU terminals allow 6 operators to enter data simultaneously. Data entered on to disc is then transferred to magnetic tape.

Purchasing Department microcomputer

Main store of 64 kilobytes. Twin 5¼-inch mini floppy discs with storage capacity of ¾ megabytes (million characters). Matrix printer of 120 characters per second.

These specifications relate to the system at the Westpool site only. Factories throughout the organisation have their own facilities, in most cases very similar to the Westpool installation. A number of items of equipment are also rented from the Post Office (British Telecom) to allow terminals to communicate with computers.

The computer operators have lists of jobs which have to be run. Many of these are done at regular intervals, eg the payroll programs are run every Tuesday. Once the data for these jobs has been prepared the operator has to check his instructions for running the job (called **documentation**). This will usually include a diagram, called a **systems flowchart**, which shows which equipment and data are required (see below).

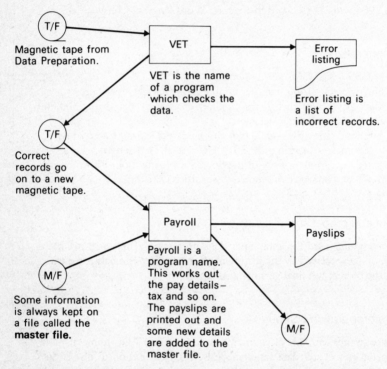

A typical systems flowchart

When a job has to be run the operator types in the name of the job on a VDU called the **operator's console**. The central processing unit will then transfer the programs from a magnetic disc, where they are usually stored, to its main memory. This program will then start to run (**execute** is the technical term for this). The program will then take in data, usually from magnetic tape as in the case of the VET program. In some cases another tape unit may be required for the results of this process. The Data VET program, for example, checks each of the items of data for errors (yet another check!). Any records which have no errors are recorded on another magnetic tape while those with errors are printed out on high-speed printers. The operators then have to take the error listing to Data Control so that they can find out what the errors are and correct them.

Some processes require data to be taken from tapes and stored on magnetic discs. This means that lots of different pieces of equipment are required for each job, eg disc units for storing data and programs, magnetic tape units for storing data and printers for producing the results.

All of this computing equipment requires controlled operating conditions. The machines are all electrical and have to be connected to each other and to the mains supply and they all give out heat. A false floor in the computer room allows all of the connecting cables to run underneath it and out of the way and also allows cold air to be brought in to control the temperature. The humidity (amount of moisture in the atmosphere) also has to be controlled and the air should be filtered to prevent dust from getting on to the sensitive equipment. This meant that when the first computer was supplied a large amount of air conditioning and filtration equipment had to be installed, causing major inconvenience within Fashion 85.

The software

The *software* for the Fashion 85 computer system, like that for Jean Byer's system, comes in two different types. The *systems software* was bought with the computer. It is stored permanently on magnetic discs and the processor transfers it to its main memory when required. These programs are far more sophisticated than those on the microsystem and there are more of them.

To control the system and keep track of what each piece of equipment is doing a program called the **operating system** is supplied. This means that the human operator can give this program a list of jobs required and the data required for each job and the computer can then carry on with the minimum of help. It will work through the **job queue**, sometimes working on several jobs at the same time, and it will inform the human operator of what is going on, what discs and tapes are required and other details. Messages produced on the console device will tell the operator when the paper needs changing on the printer or when magnetic tapes need changing. The human operator is still a very important part of the whole procedure. He must organise the jobs to be tackled (this is called **batch processing**) and make sure that all of the equipment is available to be used by the processor.

The second type of systems software programs which are extremely important are the translating programs. Over the years many different computer languages have been developed to help programmers explain to the computer exactly what is required. Engineers use their own language when working on engineering problems and to explain these problems to computers the language **FORTRAN** (FORmula TRANslator) was developed. Commercial people use a different language to sort out business problems and a language called **COBOL** (COmmon Business Oriented Language) was developed to explain commercial problems to the computer.

The problem is that the computer can only understand its own language, called **machine code**, so to understand FORTRAN programs or COBOL programs it must first translate these programs to machine code. It does this using translation programs called **compilers**. These programs are also stored on magnetic discs so that they are available to the system. When a program is loaded the operating system is told which language it is written in and it then organises the translation process using the correct compiler.

The third type of systems software supplied with the computer system is a group of programs which the operator or operating system can call on to do various tasks. These are generally grouped under the heading of **utility programs**. The Fashion 85 system has a number of these within the system, mainly used for technical operations. One will sort a file into some known order while others will organise data transfers from one device to another.

Just as the system bought by the Purchasing Department requires *applications software*, so the Data Processing Section's machine requires programs to do specific jobs. The applications programs are written for every task which the computer system has to carry out—stock control, payroll, production control and so on. Many of these programs were 'bought in' from a software house, but now Fashion 85 employs its own programming staff in the Systems Support Section.

Linking head office and the factories

The organisation of Fashion 85 has caused some problems because of the number of factories within the organisation. To work efficiently all of the factories should be supplying information to the head office at Westpool. Many ways of providing electronic data processing were examined when Ed and Tilley were originally setting up the system.

One way was to let each individual factory go its own way and computerise the systems that they wanted to computerise. This would have meant leaving the decisions to the local factory managers and would have resulted in a system called **distributed data processing**.

Another alternative was to install one massive computer at the Westpool site to provide **centralised data processing**, with all of the other factories sending data to Westpool. There were several points against the implementation of this system. It would have required a massive increase in the Westpool staff, not to mention a large rebuilding programme to accommodate the staff and equipment. Additionally, the expense of getting all of the data to Westpool would have made the system too expensive.

The system which was finally adopted for computerising Fashion 85 and which is now in operation is for each factory to have its own computer system. In some cases these systems are quite small minicomputers. These machines do most of the processing for the local sites but telephone links also exist between the factories and the Westpool site. These links can be used to transmit data from any of the computers to the main data processing system at Westpool. The computers can 'talk to each other' if data is required for particular jobs.

Another way of using the data transmission telephone link is to connect terminals to them so that data can be input to the Westpool computer from any of the other factories and the results can be sent back to that factory from Westpool. Two types of terminal device are installed with the Fashion 85 organisation for this purpose. Most terminals are visual display units but some sites have teletypes. Instead of having a screen to display information these have a built-in printer. This means that a '*hard copy*' of any results can be filed away or shown to people in other parts of the building.

This system has many advantages. By deciding from the start exactly what

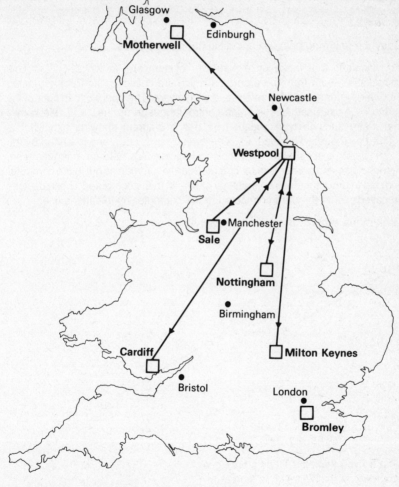

Fashion 85 data transmission network

computer equipment each factory would require Fashion 85 could buy all of the machinery from one manufacturer; this meant that they could get big discounts and a really good service. Each factory still has the benefit of electronic data processing on site and they are able to set up their computer systems to meet their own local requirements.

Head Office are very pleased with the system. Data is often required from the factories to enable long-term planning to be carried out. This data can now be transmitted to the Westpool computer for processing and the computer can then give the information required immediately. The cost of hiring the expensive data transmission equipment from British Telecom is justified because it is now used only for vital interchanges between Head Office and the other factory sites.

Exercise 23

1   Copy the following passage and fill in the blank spaces.

The machines that make up a computer system are known as .... This distinguishes them from the programs which are called .... People running computer systems are often referred to as liveware. The operator can control the system by typing instructions in job control language on the .... He knows what instructions to type because he has a diagram showing him what is required by the job. This diagram is called a .... and is written by the .... It uses special symbols to indicate files held on magnetic tape, magnetic disc and printer files for output. Some equipment is not in the computer room but in other factories so that they can 'talk' to the computer. These devices are called .... they are connected to the computer by telephone lines.

2   Look at the section of a systems flowchart below.

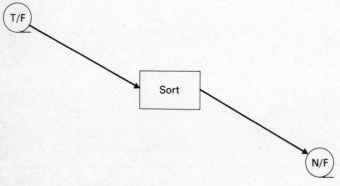

A section of a systems flowchart

a What do you think file T/F is stored on?
b What do you think file N/F is stored on?
c What is the purpose of this job?

3 Put any new words and their meanings in your Glossary.
4 Write two headings *hardware* and *software*. Put the following items under the correct heading.

a Disc unit
b Magnetic tape unit
c COBOL
d Sort routine

e CPU
f Accounts package
g Compiler
h VDU

Systems support

The Systems Support team's function is to write and maintain software. Systems Analysts examine data processing functions within the organisation with a view to making them more efficient. Usually this means writing computer programs and computerising the system but it may be that some other solution may be found—card index systems, for example. However, if the computer is to be used to make the system more efficient then the Systems Analyst designs the programs and the Programmer writes and tests them. When the programs are correct the Systems Analyst supervises the change from the old system; this includes creating the necessary files, staff training and any new methods of data capture which may be required.

When Jean Byers originally wanted to computerise the Purchasing Department's system she sought the advice of the Systems Support team. They looked at the system and the costs which might be involved and decided that while they could put the requirements on to the main computer it might be cheaper and easier to buy a *turnkey* package (computing equipment and software together) from a dealer to do the job Jean wanted. Microcomputers are quite cheap and the programs had already been written by a company specialising in this sort of thing. If the programs had had to be developed from the start by the Fashion 85 team it would have been a long and expensive process. Jean was put in touch with the company that eventually supplied her system.

Security

The Data Processing sections of all the Fashion 85 factories handle very private information. Personnel details and pay details, about which people are very sensitive, are held on the computer files. However, of more importance to the company are the details relating to the products made by Fashion 85; many other companies in the same type of business would benefit from the information on these files. This means that security is very important. Only authorised personnel, which generally means the people working there, are allowed into the Data Processing sections. They have their own keys to the main door and the Data Processing Manager's office overlooks this door. At present the manager is considering installing a special type of lock which will only open when a plastic card is inserted. Each authorised person will then be given his or her own card with a number on it. The lock 'reads' the card and if the number is correct the door opens.

The telecommunications equipment provides another method of gaining access to the computer. To use this equipment you do not have to get into the computer room. To make the equipment secure everybody with the authority to access the computer is given a code number.

When a user first tries to use the system (this is called **logging on**) the computer asks for the code number. If the correct number is typed the the computer will 'talk' to the user; otherwise the user cannot gain access to the system. The code numbers are designed so that the operating system (this is the program which actually carries out the checking) can allow different levels of access to the users. For example, people in the Personnel Department can only get access to the personnel files and so on.

Occasionally a machine goes mad and 'crashes' a disc or a tape for some reason beyond human control. If this happens it is a disaster as the data is then lost. Even worse situations can occur, such as a fire in the computer room which could cause most of the data held on *all* of the files to be lost. For this reason Fashion 85 keeps duplicate copies of all of the tapes and discs and stores them at a different site. They have also made an agreement with another local factory which has the same type of equipment so that if a major disaster does occur they can buy time on the other company's machine.

Exercise 24

1   Part of the job of the computer operator is to make copies of all the tapes and discs used. These are then sent to the Nottingham factory where they are stored. Why do you think this is done?
2   List as many security precautions as you can that are carried out by Fashion 85.
3   Fashion 85 decided that all of their factories should buy similar equipment from the same manufacturer. Write a list of advantages and disadvantages of doing this rather than letting each factory make its own decision as to what equipment to buy.
4   Add any new words and meanings to your Glossary.

Assignment 9

1   When Jean Byers was considering buying her microcomputer system she had to collect as much information on the current products as possible. She asked you to collect the information and index it for her.

Collect as much advertising material for microcomputer equipment as possible and keep it on a file. Divide the file into sections so that the information relating to each particular model is kept together. You may have one section for printers, one for computer systems, and so on. Produce an index listing the contents of your file.

2 As part of your course at Westpool College you are going to learn to program the computer. To give you some idea of what is involved you invent a simple language with a limited number of instructions (similar to a computer language). This language is to give instructions to a human computer. This means that a person could carry out a simple task just by following the instructions given.

The instructions which can be used are:

STAND	STEP UP ONE STEP
SIT	STEP DOWN ONE STEP
FORWARD ONE STEP	GET HOLD (of some object)
BACKWARD ONE STEP	RELEASE
TURN 1/4 CIRCLE LEFT	LIFT
TURN 1/4 CIRCLE RIGHT	PUSH DOWN
SIDEWAYS LEFT ONE STEP	STOP
SIDEWAYS RIGHT ONE STEP	

A simple program to get somebody out of a room may be something like:

```
    STAND
A   FORWARD ONE STEP
    IF YOU HAVE NOT REACHED THE DOOR THEN DO A
    GET HOLD OF DOOR HANDLE
    PUSH DOWN
    BACKWARD ONE STEP
    RELEASE
    SIDEWAYS LEFT ONE STEP
    FORWARD ONE STEP
    SIDEWAYS RIGHT ONE STEP
    FORWARD ONE STEP
```

Try out this program starting from some point in the room in front of the door. You may have to make some changes to allow for different methods of opening doors and other factors in the room.

Write another program explaining how to get from the door of your room to the front door of your school or college.

3 Here are the clues for the computing crossword.

Across

1 Translates data to form suitable for computer input. (8)

4 Sets of instructions. (8)

7 Operators, programmers, supervisors, are all . . . (5)

8 Small computer, but not too small. (4)

10 The computer operator . . . tapes on to tape deck. (5)

11 The device can read type. (3)

Down

1 Department dedicated to making processing easier. (2)

2 An input/output device— is this the end? (8)

3 Printers produce continuous . . . (5)

5 Looks after systems—could be a scientist. (7)

6 Name of 4 across. (8)

8 An even smaller computer. (5)

9 Magnetic—not red. (4)

9 Data processing personnel

The number of people involved in electronic data processing has increased as the number of jobs handled by the computer system has expanded. Although they are still part of the Accounts Department, Ed Sorter, the Data Processing Manager, has complete control. He works closely with Tilley Spencer and has to have Tilley's agreement if some major change is to be made, but otherwise Ed looks after the running of the section.

Ed is a distinguished looking middle-aged man who originally trained as an engineer. His interest in computing began when the company he was working for started to computerise some aspects of his work. As he became more closely involved with the computer his company retrained him as a computer programmer. Over a number of years he worked his way up with the company and was eventually appointed as a Project Leader. He was responsible for putting new applications on the computer system, arranging for new equipment and getting the programs written.

When Fashion 85 was installing their first computer system they advertised for a Data Processing Manager. This meant that the person who was to run the system would be involved from the very start and would understand exactly what was happening at every stage of the installation. Ed applied for the job because it offered a challenge and promotion from his present situation. Tilley Spencer and Hiram Clarke interviewed several candidates and were particularly impressed by Ed's qualifications and experience. He seemed to have some good ideas as to how Fashion 85 could use computing equipment so he was offered the job.

Since that time Ed has been in charge of the Computing Section which has expanded over the years to four or five times its original size. Ed is now a very important member of the management team because there are very few areas within Fashion 85 which do not rely on the computer for processing data. Even when the mainframe computer is not used it is up to Ed to advise on the best methods of carrying out data processing.

The Computing Section is split into two parts. Operations under the Operations Manager, Cardew Loader, is responsible for the day-to-day running of jobs through the computer system. This area includes Data Control and Data Preparation. The other part of the computing section is Systems Support run by the Senior Systems Analyst, Mr N Quire.

Operations

Data Control Supervisor

The Data Control Supervisor, Mags Tapper, has four data control clerks working for her. Apart from checking for errors in the batches of data delivered to Data Processing, the Section also has to keep a log of when the jobs are delivered, the time they are delivered and who delivered them. This is so that if there are any problems—a job goes missing, for example—there is a check as to when it arrived in the Section. The equipment for dealing with the output—the bursters, decollators, trimmers and guillotines—is also Mags's direct responsibility.

Mags is a middle-aged lady with a grown-up family. She realises that her position is an important one and she will tolerate no nonsense, either from the clerks or maintenance engineers. The engineers are often called in when the equipment is not running properly or has given up altogether. Their attitude is that young girls should not be allowed to operate sophisticated equipment as it is obviously outside their capabilities (like driving cars!). However, none of them would ever dare to express such a view when Mags was around or she would reprimand them soundly. At the same time she always expects the girls who work for her to give every ounce of effort. She has a very low opinion of the educational system and thinks that all young girls coming out of school these days lack the discipline to work properly but she instils this necessity into them very quickly. The result is that her department is very efficient but she is not the most popular of supervisors. She has spent all of her working life in offices and has worked her way up from being a clerk.

Data Preparation Supervisor

The Data Prep Supervisor, Vera Dijou, also worked her way up but she is a complete contrast to Mags. She started as a trainee data prep operator when she left school. At that time everybody was using punched card equipment and it was on such a system that she trained. After completing her six-month training period she stayed with the company for only two years before taking a job at Fashion 85 for more money. Within the space of three years Vera was promoted to Data Prep Supervisor.

At first many people were not very happy about her promotion, thinking that she was too young to be responsible for a section. Mr Loader, her boss, has been very pleased with her, however, and she has proved more than capable of supervising six data prep operators (they used to be called punched card girls but thought that that term sounded more like a rock band), not to mention several hundred thousand pounds worth of key-to-disc data prep equipment.

Vera is very conscientious and tends to supervise by example. She works extremely hard and because she is popular with the girls who work with her they tend to work hard too. They respect the fact that she is basically an operator like them and if they are short staffed for any reason it is not uncommon for Vera to fill in and punch data. Her job is to ensure that the data is ready for input to the computer and she makes sure that this is always done as she realises that other departments cannot accept excuses when they require information. The girls operating the data prep equipment have an extra incentive for working hard in that they are paid on piecework rates.

The Operations team

The third area of responsibility for Cardew Loader is the Operations team. This consists of two shifts, each comprising a shift leader, operator and either a junior operator or a trainee operator. These people are usually trained by the company and work their way up. There is a lot of opportunity for computer operators to become shift leaders or senior operators with other companies, which means that there is a steady turnover of computer operations staff.

Having these two shifts means that the computer can run for 16 hours a day, and with Data Control and Data Prep working normal office hours it means a steady stream of work. Data prepared and sent to the computer room for 5 pm can be run before the system closes down at 10 pm and the results can be sent to Data Control for them to deal with the following morning. The morning operations shift can then deal with what are called 'housekeeping' jobs—copying tapes and getting rid of data no longer required. A lot of testing and development is carried out in the mornings and quite often data and information may be sent to the Westpool system from one of the other factories, using their terminals.

Operations control the computer system by means of the operations console which is a special VDU. When the operators are not keying-in instructions to the system using a special language called JCL (**Job Control Language**) the screen is used either to display the status of the system, ie which jobs are running, or to pass messages from the programs which are running to the operators. These messages will tell the operator that a magnetic tape needs changing or that the printer has run out of paper.

In some cases **pre-printed** or **multi-part stationery** may be required before results can be printed out. The program will tell the operator that it is ready to print the results and will ask him to make sure that the correct paper is on the line-printer. When the operator has checked the print requirements he can tell the program to carry on printing by typing an instruction on the console.

The computer may be working on several different jobs at the same time and this means that the operators are constantly checking the console screen, changing magnetic discs and magnetic tapes. The printer ribbons often need changing and so does the paper. The computer room is generally a hive of activity and the noise of the equipment adds to the general confusion.

On Tuesdays, when the payroll is run the general air is one of panic. This is a very big job which has to be completed on time otherwise people would not get paid. This causes extra pressure because many other jobs are still being worked on by the system, and means that the operators generally hate Tuesdays.

Fashion 85 computer operators are a mixed bunch of people. They are mostly young people with a few 'O' levels each. The policy at Fashion 85 is to advertise for trainee operators and then give the applicants an aptitude test to see if they are likely to be any good at the job. They then take the best applicant and offer him a place for a probationary six-month period. At the end of that time his progress is assessed and he may be taken on as a permanent member of staff. They all know that the policy is one of internal promotion and that if they do a good job they will either be promoted within the Fashion 85 organisation or they will stand a good chance of promotion elsewhere. The result is that while some of them may be inclined to be high-spirited they generally do their jobs well.

Exercise 25

1   Make a list of the main job function of the following.

a Mags Tapper (Data Control Supervisor).
b Vera Dijou (Data Preparation Supervisor).
c Cardew Loader (Computer Operations Manager).
d Derek Minder (Computer operator).

2   What do you think the following terms mean?

a Piecework rates.
b A policy of internal promotion.
c Supervising by example.

3   Read through the passage and add any new words or phrases to your Glossary.

Systems Support

The staff of the second part of the Data Processing Section are not directly involved with the day-to-day running of the system.

Mr N Quire is the Senior Systems Analyst in charge of the Systems Support team. He is a highly intelligent man with a degree in computer science and a lot of experience, starting as a programmer and later as a Systems Analyst. He has another Systems Analyst and two programmers working with him.

At the moment they are fortunate in having a trainee programmer, a young man who has been working for several years with Fashion 85 as a computer operator. He was extremely keen and seemed to have the makings of a programmer, so Cardew Loader discussed the situation with Ed Sorter and Norman Quire and they decided to offer the young man a job as trainee programmer. This entails a lot of hard work and he has to go on training courses and attend night classes if he wants to make the best of this opportunity and be of value to the company.

Systems Analyst

The job of the Systems Analyst is a complicated one. Whenever a situation is thought to be inefficient a Systems Analyst may be brought in to examine the system and see if it can be made more efficient. The analytical part of the job involves discussing the system with the managers to get some idea of what is required of it. The Analyst examines the existing system in minute detail by observing the people involved and by interviewing them. Sometimes he will ask people to fill in questionnaires or time people as they carry out tasks involved in their jobs.

The Analyst will then produce a report based on his findings and he will find methods of improving the system. The **outline system** is presented to the management as a feasibility study and after discussions it will be decided how the actual system will be implemented and what it will involve.

A **detailed system design** is the next stage and this will involve designing new forms and finding a new method of data collection and processing. If the computer is to be used then the Systems Analyst must decide exactly what the computer is to do. He will decide what the output will be and then design a method of collecting and processing the data to achieve that result. He will use a variety of charts and diagrams to help him to explain to the management and the programmers exactly what is required. His job does not finish, however, once the system is designed.

When the forms have been printed and the programs have been written the Systems Analyst supervises the implementation. He may have to make changes to his system at this stage because sometimes things which work correctly on paper may not work quite so well in practice. It is for this reason that a computerised system is not used as soon as it is finished. Instead the old system is used at the same time as the computerised system for a time. This is called **parallel running** and it means that the results from the computerised system can be compared with those from the previous one to make sure that no errors are being introduced. This also gives an opportunity to compare the performance of the two systems and find out if the new one really is more efficient.

Eventually the Systems Analyst can supervise the change to the new system and unless something drastic goes wrong he will then be looking for a new project upon which to work.

Computer programmer

The job of the computer programmer is to convert the ideas of the Systems Analyst to a set of instructions which can be understood by the computer. This can be a very complicated task as many programs are long and complicated and this often means that all of the programmers have to work together as a team on a single job. The parts of the program then have to be tested before they can be put together and the Systems Analyst then works with the team to get the program working.

A large part of the programmer's job is to maintain existing software. This does not mean that programs break down and require oiling but that they become out of date. For example, changes in the method of working out income tax may be introduced by the Government and this will mean rewriting the wages programs. Programs are often changed to make them more efficient. Writing changes into programs is what software maintenance is all about.

The reason for the number of computer languages in use is that the computer is used for many different purposes. Different languages have been designed specifically for each application, and programmers may have to be able to write in several of them. The Fashion 85 team use COBOL for most of the programs but some of the more mathematical programs are written in FORTRAN and ASSEMBLER. This means that the programmers have to know several of these languages.

The strange thing about the programmer's job in Fashion 85 is that he very rarely actually comes into direct contact with the computer. He will write programs on forms called **coding sheets**. These, together with specially designed **test data**, go to Data Prep to be transferred to magnetic tape. The operators then load the tape and run the programs with the test data. The results are returned to the programmer and he can decide whether the program has worked or where changes have to be made to make it work. The alterations can be written on coding sheets and sent off to Data Prep once again.

The programmer may also have to write some of the **documentation** or the instructions telling the operator exactly how to run the program and what data is required.

Exercise 26

1   Here is a list of people who work for Fashion 85:

a Programmer
b Data Prep operator
c Systems Analyst
d Data Control clerk
e Computer operator

Copy out the following list of tasks and say who on the above list would carry them out.

- Checking batch totals
- Loading magnetic tapes on to tape decks
- Verifying data
- Receiving data into the department
- Writing feasibility reports
- Changing paper on printers
- Interviewing people involved in data capture in the factory
- Translating specifications into programs

2 A Systems Analyst has to find out everything he can about an existing system before he can make it more efficient. Discuss the methods which you think he might use to do this and then write these down as a list.

3 A Systems Analyst has a very complicated job and it demands a lot of different skills. Make a list of all of those which you think would be required by a person applying for such a job with Fashion 85.

4 Bring your Glossary up to date.

Assignment 10

1   A management meeting is coming up soon and they are going to discuss the organisation of Fashion 85. Frank Stamper asks if you will draw up an organisation chart to show the positions of everyone involved in the Data Processing Section from Ed Sorter to the clerks and operators in the section.

2   Several people are due to leave Fashion 85 in the near future and the Personnel Department is discussing the requirements for replacements. You happen to be visiting the Department during the conversation and your opinion is asked on an unofficial basis. They are discussing the sort of attributes they would expect of a programmer. So far they have got:

a   experience in programming
b   ability to think logically
c   ability to communicate his/her thoughts
d   well qualified
e   aged 25 or over

Copy out this list and discuss these qualities with the other members of your group. Add as many relevant items as you think of to complete the list.

Write similar lists giving the qualities you would expect of people filling the following vacancies:

a   Data Control clerk
b   Data Prep operator

3 Fashion 85 use some Post Office (British Telecom) services to link their terminals into the Westpool computer system. They are thinking of putting in some extra equipment and you are asked to do a preliminary check to see what is available. Make a list of the different services available under the name *Datel* (a starting point may be the telephone directory).

10 File processing

The main function of most data processing systems is to collect data items, keep them up to date and in some useful order and then produce information from them. The actual tasks involved in file maintenance and processing are always the same but the methods used to carry them out depend on the type of file and the medium on which it is stored. Two main methods of data processing may be used.

1   Files held in human readable form may be processed manually. Card index or document files are looked after by people. If data has to be changed or information taken from the files then somebody has to carry out these tasks. A large proportion of data processing is carried out in this way.
2   Files held in machine readable form may be processed electronically. Magnetic tape or magnetic disc files have to be read by machines usually under the control of a computer. The computer program gives instructions to the hardware to explain exactly what processes are to be carried out and how these tasks should be done. To be of use the information must eventually be converted into some human readable form and the computer programs also control this process. Computers are so fast that it is worth the large amount of money that they cost to get most of the routine filing tasks carried out automatically. They are excellent at carrying out routine jobs but not very good at 'one off' jobs (the job that only has to be carried out once and never again).

Quite often it is useful to be able to get most of the work done automatically by computer but still be able to carry out some manual processing if it is required. Media like *magnetic stripe cards* and *magnetic ink characters* allow the users to be able to choose whether processes are carried out manually or by machine. The operations which have to be carried out on files can be divided into different types.

Sorting

A file which is organised in some known order is easier to deal with than one which is in random order. The time spent on sorting files into order is saved over and over again when other processes are carried out on the file.

The records on the file may be organised in many different ways. A customer file in which the records contain the customer's name, address, account number and credit rating may be in:

1 **alphabetical order,** depending on the customer's name;
2 it may be organised **geographically**, with all of the customers living in the same area being grouped together;
3 or it may be in **numerical order**, depending on account number.

In any of these cases the order can go in **ascending order** (starting with the lowest value and going up to the highest) or **descending order** (starting with the highest). The order can be specified by giving the **key field** and the direction. If the customer file is arranged so that the records go from the lowest account number to the highest account number then the **key field** is said to be the account number, and it is in ascending order.

Quite often it is useful to organise large files on more than one key. A personnel file may be arranged in ascending order of *surname* within *department* (see below).

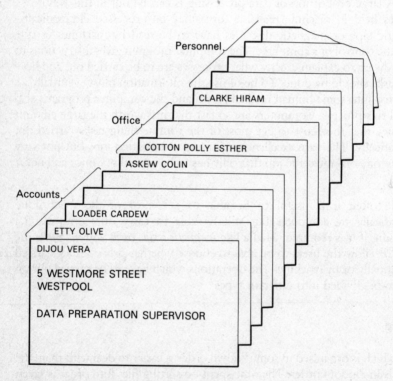

Organisation of Fashion 85 personnel file

In some cases different departments want the same file but they each want it arranged in a different order. The customer file may be extremely useful to the Sales Department if it is arranged in alphabetical order of surname, whereas the Accounts Department find that it is more useful if they arrange it numerically on account number. The Transport Department could find it very useful if it was arranged in geographical order. Each department may have its own copy of the file arranged as required.

This ordering of files is so important that computer systems usually have several programs which sort files, and most jobs will incorporate a sort stage before any other processes are carried out. This is the type of activity which takes a very long time to do manually but which can be done very quickly by computerised methods.

Exercise 27

1 Explain why the Transport, Accounts and Sales Departments may each require the customer file in a different order.

2 Obtain a set of small pieces of card (one for each member of your class). On each card write the name of one of your classmates (*surname first*). Shuffle the cards. Each card represents a record on a file. (The other information which could be held on file has been left out to avoid confusion.) The file should now be in random order. Now rearrange your file:

a in ascending order of surname; then
b in descending order of surname.

How many different ways of carrying out this task can you find? Discuss the various methods used with the rest of your group. Can any methods achieve the end result quicker than others?

3 When computers are used to sort very large files it is convenient for the program to look at a small number of records at a time. Many different ways have been invented for computers to sort files, some more efficient than others. Use your class file prepared for Question **2** to try the following method used by computers.

Shuffle the cards to produce a random file to start with. Turn all of the cards face downwards (these would normally be on a magnetic tape or disc anyway). Arrange the cards so that they are in a line. You are now going to sort them into ascending order so that they look like this:

1		2		3		4

Work through the following instructions very carefully.

a Pick up the first two cards (the computer program would look at the first two records).
b If the cards are in the correct order put them down again (face downwards). If not, swap the two cards around and then put them face down.

c Pick up the right-hand card which you have just put down and the one next to it.

d If the cards are in the correct order put them down again (face downwards). Otherwise swap the cards around and then put them down again.

e Repeat stages (*c*) and (*d*) until you have checked the whole file.

f You have now completed **one pass** of the file (from beginning to end). If during this pass you have swapped any cards then go to stage (*a*) and make another pass. Otherwise you have sorted the file.

g Turn all of the cards over. They should now be in order.

Note: a problem may arise if two people have the same surname. You must decide what to do if this should arise.

This may seem a very slow way of sorting files but remember that the computer can carry out each stage very quickly (in a few thousandths of a second).

Updating

Keeping a file up to date may involve three separate stages.

1 Adding records to a file. The Fashion 85 personnel file has to have extra records added every time somebody new starts working for the company. It is important that these records are added in the correct place to keep the file in order.

2 Deleting records from the file. As people leave Fashion 85, for example, their records are removed from the personnel file.

3 Changing information on the records in the file. This is a very common way of updating files. People move house so the address field of their record has to be changed.

With manual file handling updating is a question of finding the records and taking the appropriate action. When computerised files are updated the process is more complicated and several stages may be involved (see the diagram opposite).

First of all the details of the changes may have to be put on to magnetic tape by Data Prep (this especially applies if a large number of records are involved). This tape file may be called the **changes file** (in some cases it may be known as the **transaction file**). The next stage is to sort this file so that the records are in the same order as the file which is to be changed. This is carried out by a *sort program* which puts the sorted file on to a new magnetic tape or a disc. A program which carries out the update procedure (called a **merge update**) then reads the changes file and the file is changed and produces a new file. It is usual for this program to print a list of all of the changes that have been made at the same time so that any humans involved in the system can see what has happened to the file.

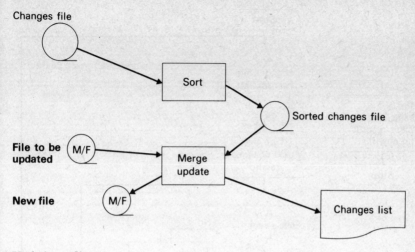

Updating a file

If the file update involves a small number of records then it may be possible to type the information in on a visual display unit if the computer program allows for this. This type of processing is often required in places like banks where it is important that files containing bank account information must be updated without any delay (the technical term for this is **on-line transaction processing**).

A special type of updating occurs when the file has no records to start with, ie the file does not exist. In this case the only updating procedure which can be carried out is that of adding records to the file. This is called **creating** a file.

Exercise 28

1 Does it matter in which order the three file update processes (*add, delete, change*) are carried out? If it does, what is the best order?

2 If one of the girls working for Fashion 85 gets married then her personnel record will have to be updated. This could be a complicated process, possibly requiring three changes to her record and a change in the file structure. Discuss what these changes may be and how this situation could be processed. List the changes required on the personnel record.

3 Obtain three more pieces of card. On two of them write the names of two people in your group (remember surname first). On one of these cards put a letter D and on the other put a letter C and a star. Write Keen U R on the third card and a letter A. These three cards will represent your changes file and the letters represent transaction codes (D for *delete*, C for *change* and A for *add*). Arrange these cards in alphabetical order of surname (the same order as your class file).

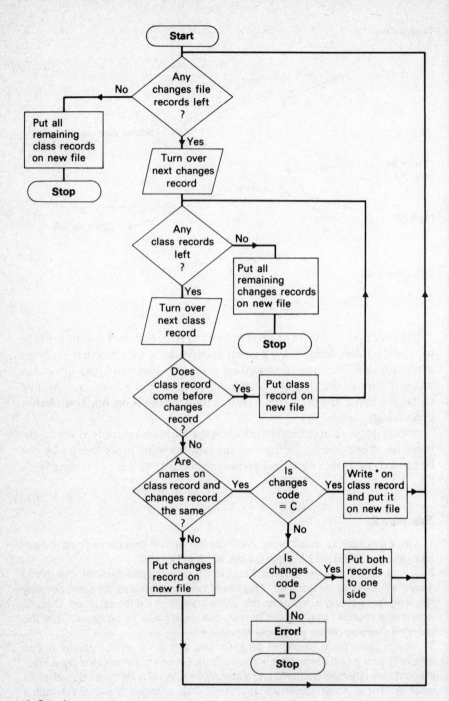

A flowchart

Look at the **flowchart** on page 124. These are often used to explain data processing tasks. From the *start* box do as the flowchart says until you reach the end and you should then have updated your file in the same way that a computer program carries out the task.

Start with your class file and changes file in separate piles face downwards in front of you. The new file will be a third pile created from these two. The changes will be to add records, delete records, and change records (write an * on the card). Begin at the *start* box and follow the arrows, doing as it says at each stage. At the diamond boxes go in the direction indicated by the answer you give to the question.

Searching

The method of finding a particular record on a file is governed very much by the medium on which the file is stored and the method of organisation.

If the file is in random order or, more likely, if the file is sorted on one key and we wish to find information in a different field then the only way to search the file is serially. For example, the personnel file is in alphabetical order and we want to find a record but we only have the works number. The only way to find such a record is to start at the beginning of the file and examine each record in order until the required one is found. Files held on magnetic tape always have to be searched in this way. The program which searches tape files is given a **search key** by the operator. The tape is read record by record and the fields are compared with the search key. When the required record is found, information can be extracted from it and this is usually printed out.

When the file is organised in such a way that the search key is the same as the field on which the file is sorted then more efficient methods of searching can quite often be used. A card index file containing a list of names and addresses in alphabetical order of surname can be **accessed** randomly. This means that you can start looking at the records at any point without having to start at the beginning and reading through. If a Mr Yuill's record is required then it would be reasonable to start looking towards the end of the file. Similarly, that of Mr Maynard is probably going to be near the middle.

Magnetic disc files have this ability to be accessed randomly, and computer programs searching these files can use a system called a **binary chop**. The required record is given to the program which then finds the mid-point of the file to be searched. The key field is compared with the required record and if they are not the same the program decides which half of the file the record must be in. The program then finds the mid-point of that half of the file and repeats the process until the required record is found. Fewer comparisons are required by this type of search and therefore it can be much faster than the linear search.

Exercise 29

1 Write the headings *Random access* and *Serial access*. Put the following under the appropriate headings.

a Scroll
b Book
c Card index
d Magnetic tape file
e LP record
f Pre-recorded tape cassette
g Magnetic disc file
h Document file

2 Suppose your class records contained an address field and an age field and they were organised in ascending order on surname. Say whether you would use a serial search or a binary search to find:

a the age of a member of your class, given her name.
b the age of a member of your class, given only her address
c the address of a member of your class, given her name
d the name of a member of your class, given only her address

3 Take your class file and perform a binary search on it by carrying out the following.

a Choose the name of one of the members of your class. It is this record you are going to find.
b Divide the file in half and examine the middle record.
c If this record is the one that is required you have finished. If not, carry on.
d Decide which half of the file the record should be in and put the other half to one side.
e Take the remaining half of the pack.
f Treat this half as a new file and repeat the instructions from b.

Assignment 11

1 Create a card index file by copying the first ten records from the customer file (see Appendix 2 on page 140) on to cards.
2 Sort the file into ascending order on *customer name*.
3 The Sales Department have to make several changes to the customer file. New orders are received from:

- *Tubman Fashions*   Stockton, Cleveland
- *Rem Modes*   Acklam, Middlesborough, Cleveland
- *Davos Dresses*   Sunderland, Tyne and Wear
- *Armstrongs Ltd*   Aycliffe, Co Durham
- *Willis Fashions*   Darlington, Co Durham
- *Bells Boutique*   Hartlepool, Cleveland
- *Under Twenty*   Northallerton, N Yorks.

These are given account numbers between 9213 and 9219 and a credit limit of £500.

Unfortunately letters have also been received to say that *E Whatmore* and *B Fiske* are no longer trading. *Everard Presser* have written to say that they have now moved to *Kendal* in Cumbria and the Accounts Department have suggested that C M Lomas's credit limit should be increased to £500.

Update your card index to include these amendments.

4 An enquiry has been made as to the credit rating of customer account number 4578. How can the information be obtained from the card index file?

If the file was held on magnetic disc and a program was written to obtain the relevant information, how could the program find the credit rating given:

a the customer's name
b the customer's account number?

11 Everyday data processing

In our everyday lives companies and organisations present us constantly with data. We process this to obtain information which will affect our actions. This data may be presented in a variety of ways, some of which we may not even be aware of. Quite often we are at the end of a long data processing system. We are users or customers of systems and as such often support quite large data processing networks. Putting money into a bank or building society is typical of this situation.

Typical methods of presenting data to people so that they can quickly extract useful information are **tables**, **lists**, **files** and diagrams in the form of **graphs** or **charts** (see below and on pages 129 and 130).

```
┌─────────────────────────────────┐
│           MENU                  │
│                                 │
│   Tea              25p          │
│   Coffee           20p          │
│   Fish & chips     £1.20        │
│   Sausage & chips  95p          │
│   Beans & chips    £1.00        │
│                                 │
└─────────────────────────────────┘
```

A list

```
Banks A H, 39 Ferns Cres, Ferns Est ................Hartlepool 62449
Banks A H, 32 Hawkshead Rd .............................Redcar 6915
Banks A H, 17 Jervaulx Rd, Morton-on-Swale........N'thallerton 3051
Banks A H, 30 Whitehouse Rd, Billingham .......... Stockton 554815
Banks A H, 1 Woodside, Leyburn...................Wensleydale 22571
Banks A J, 12 Dale St, New Marshe......................Redcar 2990
Banks A J, 181 Eldon St ...........................Darlington 56449
Banks A J, 25 Leicester Rd, Norton.................Stockton 559659
Banks A J, 8 Lincoln Rd ..........................Hartlepool 871247
Banks A J, 86 Lincoln Rd ............................. Redcar 78617
Banks A J, 19 Ormesby Cres, Romanby..............N'thallerton 4851
Banks A J.F, 2 Church Fm, Redmarshall.............Stillington 732
Banks A K, Hollycroft, Croft Heads,.....................Thirsk 23105
```

A file

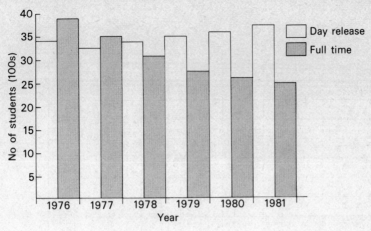

A chart

Exercise 30

1 When you walk into a café and sit down one of the things that you must do is to process the data on the menu. Write a list of the questions you might ask yourself in order to carry out this data processing.

2 You have found a purse with some money in it and you want to contact the owner. All you have to identify her is a telephone number written on a piece of paper which you found inside. Explain why it would be difficult, if not impossible, to trace the person using the telephone directory.

3 Examine the graph of student enrolments. What information can you get about the numbers of students on day release compared with those on full time courses? Discuss the trends in student enrolments with the members of your class and see if you can arrive at a conclusion as to why the graph is the shape it is.

4 I want to catch a train from Sunderland to London on the 4th of June. Using the extract from the timetable on page 130 could you write down the time of a train leaving at around 4.00 pm. Also write down whether this train has a restaurant or a buffet.

Assignment 12

Choose one of the topics from the list below. Research the topic and produce a report giving the required information. Keep a log to record details of any visits made, even if the results do not help a great deal. You should record the date of the visit, place visited, the name of the person contacted and a note relating to the results of the visit, eg gained a lot of useful information.

Read carefully the *Notes for guidance* when you prepare your report.

Scotland, North East England, Yorkshire and Humberside to London

Mondays to Saturdays

Table 26

		A SX ✕⊝ 🍴	A SO 🍴	SX ✕⊝	■ B ✕⊝		■ SX ✕⊝	C SO ✕⊝	🔲	D SX	SX 🍴	SO 🍴	E 🍴	🔲	H ✕⊝	J 🍴
241	Aberdeen	d														
241	Stonehaven	d														
241	Montrose	d														
241	Arbroath	d														
241	Dundee	d														
241	Leuchars	d														
241	Cupar	d														
241	Kirkcaldy	d														
241	Inverkeithing	d														
228	Glasgow Queen Street	d					11 49	11 49								
	Edinburgh	47 d				14 25		12 35	12 35							
	Drem	47 d				14 50		12 51	12 51							
	Dunbar	47 d				15 02		13 22	13 22							
	Berwick-upon-Tweed	47 d				15 34	14 12	14 12	14 12							
	Newcastle	47 a				16 46	14 35	14 35	14 35							
							14 00	14 00	14 00							
41	Sunderland	d	15 39	15 39	15 45		15 15	15 15	15 15					15625		
	Newcastle	d	16 13	16 16	16 35											
	Chester-le-Street	d	16 29	16 32	16 48		16 06	16 06								
	Durham	a	16 31	16 34	16 50		16 58	16 58						17616		
			16 52	16 55	17 07		16 15	16 15						16 45 16 53		
	Darlington	a														
41	Hartlepool	d			16h01			17 00	17 00	17 08				17 26 17 35		
41	Stockton	d			16h21		17 29	17u15		17 23				17 23 17 50		
41	Middlesbrough	d			16 29			17 33		17 32				17 41 17 59		
	Darlington	d	16 55 16 56		17 09		16h01 16 42	16 42		17 34				17 42		
	Northallerton	d					16h21 17 03	17 03						18 03		
	Thirsk	d			17 41		16 29 16 52	16 52						17h01		
	York	a	17 36 17 37				17 17 17 31	17 34 ← 17 33						17h21		18 15
							17 33	17 43						17 27		18 31
31	Scarborough	a		18 43	18 43		18 03	18 06 18 10	19 14					18 04		18 41
31	Leeds	a		18 21	18 21		18 58									19 08
31	Sheffield	a	18 57 18 57	19u18			20u07	20u07						18 43		
31	Scarborough	d		16 35 16 35	16 35 16 35		17u05	17u05			18 11 18 14	18 11 18 14		19 19		20 08
	York	d	17 42 17 47	17 42 17 47			18 04	18 08			18 25 18 28	18 25 18 28				20 19
	Selby	d		18 04							18 46 18 49	18 46 18 49				2014·3
	Doncaster	a	18 12 18 27	18 12 18 27												

A table

Topics

Bus tickets
Tickets are issued to passengers travelling on buses as proof that they have paid their fares. Find out how the system works.

Vehicle licensing system
Every motor vehicle used on public roads in this country must have a current road fund licence. The records relating to vehicles are kept on computer files at the Driver and Vehicle Licencing Centre in Swansea. It is, however, possible to tax a vehicle at a post office or a regional tax office.

What information is required before a Post Office can issue a licence? How is the information recorded and what happens to it? What information is recorded on the licence?

College enrolment
When a person enrols for a course at college certain information is required. Each student fills in an enrolment form which goes to the College Office.

What information is recorded? How is this information used? What happens if a student changes courses?

Current account system
A current account with a bank allows the customer to pay bills by writing cheques. Explain how the system works.

What information is recorded on the cheque? What information is added to the cheque? How is the information used? What happens if a cheque book is lost? What information does the bank require before issuing a cheque book? How does the bank keep the customer informed as to the state of his/her account?

Building society deposit account
A deposit account with a building society allows the customer to save money and the society pays interest on the amount saved.

What information is required by the society before an account can be opened? What information is recorded when money is paid into the account? What information is required before money can be withdrawn from an account?

Credit card system
A credit card allows the holder to buy goods and pay for them over a period of time. Some of the cards are issued by banks, eg Barclaycard, Access, some by private companies, eg Diners Club, American Express. Find out how the system works.

Who would be allowed to have a credit card? Are any checks made on the customer? What information is passed between a supplier of goods or services and a customer when a credit card transaction is carried out? What happens if a credit card is lost? How can a customer be prevented from running up extremely large bills which he may not be able to pay?

Notes for guidance

1 Keep a log of visits.

- When?
- Where?
- Who did you see?
- Result?

2 Outline the system examined. Explain briefly the purpose of the system and how it worked.
3 Describe the information held by the system and the reasons for holding it.
4 State the method of recording information. Give examples of any forms used where possible.
5 Explain any methods of detecting and dealing with errors in the system.
6 Explain how the information is used in the system.
7 What happens if the information needs changing, eg prices go up, somebody moves house?
8 What conclusions are there? Could the system be improved or simplified? Is information collected for no real purpose? Does the system work?

12 Future developments

The technology now exists to change our lives radically. We are living through a revolution which is every bit as important as the Industrial Revolution. Future developments can only be imagined but existing developments point to what it might be like.

Word processing

The typewriter is being replaced by word processors. These are computers which have programs to deal with text in the form of letters, reports and other documents. The operator can create a document on a VDU screen, correct it and store it on magnetic disc to be recalled and printed as it is required. The only time a printed copy of that document exists is when it is perfect and it has to be sent to another person.

If the document has to be changed then the alterations can be made to the stored copy, which means that no retyping is necessary. The format of documents can be re-arranged, with changed tab settings and different margins, without the need for retyping.

Many time-consuming jobs can be tackled automatically. Text may be right justified (have a straight right margin, as in a book) with no extra time involved. Centred headings may be inserted by typing the heading and instructing the machine to centre it. One task which may have to be carried out is to send a document to a number of people. A list of the names of the people can be *merged* with the document at print time and each copy of the document is produed with a different person's name on it.

Word processing systems are becoming more sophisticated and cheaper. Some systems now include dictionaries to check and even correct spelling, and even maths packages to allow calculations to be carried out automatically. This will eventually mean that typists will become word-processor operators whose machines will allow them to be far more efficient producing high-quality work with the absolute minimum of retyping.

1 Find out what the following terms mean when applied to word-processing systems.

a Stand alone
b Shared resource
c Thin window display
d Full screen machine

2 Collect information on word-processing systems and from it make a list of all the functions which can be carried out by word processor.

Voice recognition

Meat inspectors in an abbatoir in Australia presented their management with an interesting data processing system. Their job involved inspecting the inside and outside of carcasses of freshly-slaughtered lambs for defects. These defects fell into several categories and, depending upon what the defects were, the meat was passed as A1 and suitable for export through to unfit for human consumption. A note of the defects had to be made on a record sheet for that particular animal and the record sheets were then sent to a computer centre which carried out further data processing tasks.

The problem was that the record sheets were not in a very pleasant state after the meat inspectors had handled them (they could not wash their hands between inspecting each animal). A solution was found with a system called **Voice recognition**.

The inspectors were supplied with microphones plugged into a special 'black box' which was in turn connected to the computer. When the meat inspectors named defects as they inspected a carcass the computer recognised the word and added it to the animal's record. No messy pieces of paper were then required and the system became far more efficient.

Voice output

The prevention of accidents is an area where large amounts of money have been spent on research. One outcome of this research is a series of audio warning signals to which drivers can respond without having to look at a control.

A voice synthesiser is connected to a computer. The computer takes a signal, say, from a sensor on the petrol tank, processes the signal and the voice synthesiser says 'You are running out of petrol.' With this system the driver gets the message without having to look at warning lights, gauges or dials.

The computer can deal with input from many parts of the car and it is the aim of the companies producing such systems that in the near future the car may be driven to a garage for a service and it will be able to tell the mechanics what is wrong with it!

The electronic office

The office of the future will probably use the technology now available in different ways, as well as extending its present uses.

Filing cabinets may disappear completely. A central computer could be used for all filing. The typewriter may be completely replaced by some form of computer terminal which is used to carry out file entry and interrogation. Messages may be switched from one terminal to another without the need for printing them on paper—all internal mail and memos could be handled in this way. The computer could also file any messages which may be required in the future. The system could be made secure so that messages could only be displayed on terminals after typing in a code number, thus restricting access only to those people with the correct code number.

The manager in his office could be informed by his voice output terminal that a message had been received for him. He could then display the message on the screen and, depending on the information, could file it for future reference or destroy it. If he wanted to send a message to a company not on the computer network then he could dictate the letter to the terminal using voice input. The computer would then display it on the terminal, allowing alterations and corrections to be made. When the information is correct the manager would then ask the computer to print and send it.

In this situation printed copies of documents will only be produced when they are absolutely necessary, which will usually mean when the person to whom the document is addressed is not on the computer network. This means that in future we may see the **paperless office**, incorporating computer networks (two or more computers communicating with each other), word processing, voice input and voice output.

Exercise 32

1 Large companies have to send a lot of information internally (from one department to another). Make a list of all of the internal documents that you can think of, eg memos.
2 List all of the stages involved in sending a letter from Hiram Clarke at Fashion 85 in Westpool to the head of Production at Fashion 85 in Bromley.
3 List the stages involved in sending the same letter electronically, using the Fashion 85 computer system. Assume that Hiram Clarke and the head of Production in Bromley have computer terminals in their offices.
4 Discuss the advantages and disadvantages of having a paperless office.

The cashless society

Over the last few years money as we know it has changed. Cheques, giro and credit cards are becoming more common and in many cases money is no longer required to obtain goods and services. The payment in this case becomes a data-processing exercise.

For example, one person wants to pay a second person for goods provided. The first person informs his bank of the amount and who is to be paid, and the bank then changes the data relating to the bank accounts of the persons involved. The first person's account balance is decreased and the second person's is increased. No money has actually changed hands and the chances are that the actual transaction has been carried out in a computer system at the banks concerned. The number of transactions carried out in this way in the future will increase.

A possible situation which could occur is that most people will have bank accounts and will be issued with plastic cards like credit cards. Each card will contain the person's name and bank account number. Shops and stores will have advanced point of sales terminals, connected to the bank computer as well as to the shop's own system. When a customer buys something the shop assistant will put the card into a slot in the terminal and type in the amount due. (If bar codes are used she may not even have to do this.) The amount will then be deducted from the customer's account and added to the shop's account. The computer system could also perform security checks to make sure that the card had not been stolen or lost.

Small shops may not be able to afford expensive terminal equipment but in this case specially adapted push-button telephones with built-in card readers may be used. The shopkeeper merely inserts the customer's card and uses the buttons to key in the amount owing. The bank computer at the other end of the telephone line carries out the necessary security checks and then transfers the money from the customer's balance to the shop's balance. This system would dispense completely with the need for cash to be used.

Home computer systems

Most homes now have television sets and many also have telephones. The Post Office (British Telecom) and the television companies have systems whereby the television set may be used to receive information other than normal television programmes. **Ceefax** (BBC) and **Oracle** (IBA) are systems which enable modified television sets to have access to pages of information (like a magazine). These give news bulletins, farming information, entertainment information, weather reports, recipes and so on.

The system offered by British Telecom is called **Prestel** and it requires slightly more sophisticated equipment but it allows the user to turn his television set into a computer terminal and have access to a computer over the telephone lines. Users can also use the central computer to pass information from one Prestel terminal to another.

The microcomputer has reached a stage in its development and a price where many people are installing them at home. This allows them to learn about how computers work, to learn computer programming or to use them to play video games. The home computer is now a reality.

Experiments are being carried out to combine microcomputers with the teletext systems (Ceefax, Oracle and Prestel). Programs written and tested on one computer may be transmitted, using teletext systems, to other computers. This means that home computers may be networked (linked). The home computer could then be used to help with homework for educational purposes or connected to the company's computer to allow people to do more of their work at home. Letters could be sent from house to house or from company to company without the need to write anything down—the ultimate electronic mail.

These developments are all possible—some of them already exist in small experimental systems. They are changing our way of life already and there is no doubt that they will continue to do so—only time will tell.

Assignment 13

Nobody can accurately predict the future. We can only look at present developments and suggest what might happen. Many people have written science *fiction* stories only to find that they rapidly become science *fact*. Our views about what might happen will be coloured by all sorts of information sources—television programmes, books and magazine articles, to mention just a few.

Imagine that you are working for Fashion 85 in 20 years' time. Discuss the situation with your class and then write a description of the office—what it might look like and what the work might entail. You may decide that work patterns may change to the extent that you work from home, in which case explain how this might operate.

Use whatever material you can find to give you ideas but the description should be *your* idea of what it will be like.

Appendix 1 **Extract from Office Supplies catalogue**

Envelopes

C6		per 1000
06012	manilla plain	£2.35
06046	manilla window	£3.00
06048	business parchment self seal	£4.04

Long bankers		per 1000
06036	commerce bond white	£4.14
06072	savetime parchment window	£5.92
06083	64 mill bond white	£4.55

DL		per 1000
06014	manilla plain	£2.82
06029	manilla window	£3.40
06053	Croxley script white	£4.95

Wage pockets		per 1000
08013	2295, $4\frac{1}{4} \times 3\frac{1}{4}$ printed 'Wages Detail'	£2.25
08015	2296, $4\frac{1}{4} \times 3\frac{1}{4}$ plain	£2.14

Sundries

Bulldog Clips		per 12
21040	$\frac{3}{4}$ in	19p
21050	2 in	29p
21035	3 in	71p

paper clips		per 1000
21006	large lipped	30p
21007	large plain	30p
21008	small lipped	24p
21009	small plain	24p

Bic Crystal pens fine point		per 12
33107	black	45p
33108	blue	45p
33109	red	45p

white twine		
28033	ball medium	19p
28034	ball fine	19p
28035	Kop medium	37p
28036	Kop fine	37p

medium point		
33117	black	45p
33118	blue	45p
33119	red	45p

Paper

64 mill duplicator 18 lb		1 ream	40 reams	100 reams
10002	10×8 blue	84p	77p	75p
10003	10×8 buff	84p	77p	75p
10004	10×8 gold	84p	77p	75p
10112	13×8 blue	£1.05	99p	95p
10113	13×8 buff	£1.05	99p	95p
10114	13×8 gold	£1.05	99p	95p
10222	A4 blue	99p	92p	90p
10223	A4 buff	99p	92p	90p
10224	A4 gold	99p	92p	90p

Typing paper 18 lb

10256	10 × 8	white	84p	79p	77p
10257	A4	white	98p	92p	89p

Typing paper 21 lb

10273	10 × 8	white	98p	92p	89p
10274	A4	white	£1.17	£1.10	£1.06

Appendix 2 List of customer files

Name	Town, county	Account number	Credit limit (£)
Ida Chatter	Orpington, Kent	2345	650
H I P Spinner	York, North Yorkshire	2457	300
Everard Presser	Whitehaven, Cumbria	2145	1 000
E Whatmore	Westpool, Cleveland	3456	900
Don Lines	Gateshead, Tyne & Wear	4578	1 000
B Fiske	Grasmere, Cumbria	3421	500
Thora Bort	Wooler, Northumberland	3487	1 600
A Nutt	Berwick upon Tweed, Northumberland	3455	700
C M Lomas	York, North Yorkshire	5678	300
P McQuillan	Ashford, Kent	8899	1 500
J McGregor	Ashford, Kent	8890	500
J S Atkinson	Durham City, Durham	7788	3 000
J Blunt	Bishop Auckland, Durham	6687	900
The Dress Shop	Westpool, Cleveland	3577	1 100
R McIntosh	Ashford, Kent	8880	500
M C Goodall	Newcastle-upon-Tyne, Tyne & Wear	6678	1 000
C Macdonald	Ashford, Kent	8888	650
I Pickering	Grasmere, Cumbria	3334	800
M Llewelyn	Middlesbrough, Cleveland	5551	1 000
The Boutique	Gateshead, Tyne & Wear	7878	800
Richard Muirhead	Northallerton, North Yorkshire	4444	1 500
Sadler & Co Ltd	Darlington, Durham	6665	500
Raymond Russell & Son	Wooler, Northumberland	5454	1 000
Cliff Hanger	Tonbridge, Kent	8001	950
Go Gay Fashions	Peterlee, Durham	6543	400
Laura Large	Penrith, Cumbria	3332	900
Willie Golightly	Northallerton, North Yorkshire	4445	1 000
Ron Rowe	Scarborough, North Yorkshire	4433	500
E & F Ring & Co Ltd	Thornaby, Cleveland	5568	1 500
Snowball Clothes	Canterbury, Kent	2346	800
Albert Hall	Darlington, Durham	6689	1 400
Drake Webber Ltd	Ashington, Northumberland	3450	750
Hendersons Ltd	Harrogate, North Yorkshire	4320	1 000
Jones, Jones & Jones	Wooler, Northumberland	4564	800
Howgego Inn	Shildon, Durham	6751	750
Eileen Dover	Hartlepool, Cleveland	3333	1 300
Richardson & Kitchen Ltd	Penrith, Cumbria	3338	900
Green & Rush Ltd	Ambleside, Cumbria	3112	600
Newfashions	Northallerton, North Yorkshire	4448	1 000
Rose Bank	Whitley Bay, Tyne & Wear	7777	2 000
Tanya De Silva	Shildon, Durham	6666	1 000
The Beachwear Co Ltd	Hartlepool, Cleveland	5544	850
Tiny Tots	Whitley Bay, Tyne & Wear	7666	1 200
XL Gowns Ltd	Consett, Durham	6777	2 500

D J Wiley	South Shields, Tyne & Wear	7555	2 000
C C Doram	Hartlepool, Cleveland	3111	980
A Cass	Whitley Bay, Tyne & Wear	7222	750
Dodds, Edens & Grieveson	Orpington, Kent	2344	1 300
Alexis Leisure Wear	Sunderland, Tyne & Wear	7221	3 000
Charles De La Mott	Amble, Northumberland	3333	690
Tiffs & Toffs	Shildon, Durham	5678	950
Guys & Dolls	Gateshead, Tyne & Wear	4566	1 250
Georgina & Victoria Pratt	Sunderland, Tyne & Wear	3331	1 000
Kirsten Neil	Ambleside, Cumbria	6661	500
Saban Askwith Ltd	Sunderland, Tyne & Wear	8023	1 000
Holcroft & Holtem	Amble, Northumberland	6583	750
Lancaster Styles Ltd	Northallerton, North Yorkshire	7779	2 000
Eunice Francis Modes	Whitehaven, Cumbria	0007	2 500
Rutter & Scrafton	Peterlee, Durham	9843	500
Spencer, Armitage & Hill	Thornaby, Cleveland	7296	750
Carnaby Walker Dresses	Consett, Durham	3193	1 000
Gainey & Slimmings	South Shields, Tyne & Wear	4581	2 000
G M Payne	Ashington, Northumberland	1372	750
W B Parsons	Middlesbrough, Cleveland	9184	2 000
Harald Davison-Scott	Canterbury, Kent	2396	2 500
L Holden	Wooler, Northumberland	5521	450
Jack & Jill Fashions	Consett, Durham	4477	1 000
Little Lamb	Harrogate, North Yorkshire	1519	1 500
N C Arnold	Peterlee, Durham	1066	750
Natty Gent Suits	Grasmere, Cumbria	1812	1 000
Bancroft, Benjamin & Bland	Tonbridge, Kent	1984	500
M W Cape	Newcastle-upon-Tyne, Tyne & Wear	1973	2 000
Ida Mason	Berwick upon Tweed, Northumberland	1966	750
P Lowry Ltd	Middlesbrough, Cleveland	1789	1 000
Bib & Tucker	Durham City, Durham	4794	750
Barton's Best	Bishop Auckland, Durham	7581	2 750
J N Sheraton	Scarborough, North Yorkshire	3023	2 750
J Milner	Berwick upon Tweed, Northumberland	4711	500
M Waites	Grasmere, Cumbria	2711	1 000
Roxburgh & Hughes	York, North Yorkshire	1111	2 750
Smith & Graham	Canterbury, Kent	7123	5 000
Maughan & Jones Ltd	Ashington, Northumberland	2987	500
Bo-Peep Fashions	Hartlepool, Cleveland	2766	2 000
Wades Waistcoats	Bishop Auckland, Durham	5129	600
Smith & Son	Penrith, Cumbria	9677	4 000
Stylish Man	Consett, Durham	9967	3 000
Top Hat & Tails	Ambleside, Cumbria	9900	2 000
Smiths Ltd	Darlington, Durham	8677	1 000
Loungers Ltd	Westpool, Cleveland	3986	2 000
The Casuals Shop	Whitehaven, Cumbria	3971	1 500
Alfred Smith	Peterlee, Durham	8199	3 000
R Grimshaw	Tonbridge, Kent	9345	2 000
Man About Town	Penrith, Cumbria	1432	2 250
Taylor's Dummy	Newcastle-upon-Tyne, Tyne & Wear	4766	1 750
Perfect Fits	Amble, Northumberland	4800	3 000
Rupert Johnson	Harrogate, North Yorkshire	0654	750
L M Williams	South Shields, Tyne & Wear	2867	1 800
Denim Hills	Westpool, Cleveland	0097	3 000
Wilson Weaver Ltd	Scarborough, North Yorkshire	4912	2 500
Poole Presentations	Shildon, Durham	0337	2 000

Docherty's	Canterbury, Kent	9436	750
Dodson's Duds	Durham City, Durham	6124	1 500
Tillottson's Togs	Orpington, Kent	5124	2 750
J F L Booth	Gateshead, Tyne & Wear	2034	2 000
Paisley Prints	Thornaby, Cleveland	2544	1 000

Appendix 3 **Extract from Fashion 85 price list (trade)**

Cat/Ref No	Item	Colour	Sizes	Price
Suits/Dresses				
E 3275	Trouser suit	Brown Tweed	12 14 16 18 20	12.50
E 3276	Suit	Angora	12 14 16 18 20	13.75
E 3277	Dress	L Flowered	12 14 16 18	11.00
E 3278	Jumpsuit	Gold Lurex	10 12 14 16	7.50
E 3279	Tabard	Grey	10 12	5.50
E 3210	Tabard	Grey	14 16 18	5.75
Skirts/Trousers				
B 1673	Slacks, Flared	Brown	12 14 16 18	3.30
B 1674	Slacks, Flared	Green	12 14 16 18	3.30
B 1675	Slacks, Flared	Camel	12 14 16 18	3.30
B 1676	Slacks, Flared	Brown	20 22 24	4.50
B 1677	Slacks, Flared	Green	20 22 24	4.50
B 1678	Slacks, Flared	Navy	20 22 24	4.50
B 1679	Jeans, Cord	Green	9 11 13 15	4.25
B 1680	Jeans, Cord	Camel	9 11 13 15	4.25
B 1681	Jeans, Denim	Blue	9 11 13 15	5.80
B 1682	Culotte, Cord	Brown	9 11 13 15	3.75
B 1683	Culotte, Cord	Cream	9 11	3.75
B 1684	Culotte, Cord	Cream	13 15	4.25
Sportswear				
M 002	Anorak, Sailing	Orange	S M L	4.80
M 003	Jackets, Ski	Navy	10 12 14 16	6.50
M 004	Jackets, Ski	Navy	16 18 20	6.50
M 005	Jackets, Ski	Cream	10 12 14 16	6.25
M 006	Jackets, Ski	Green	10 12 14	6.50
M 007	Track Suit	Royal/White	S M L	7.25
M 008	Track Suit	Black/Orange	S M L	7.25
D 612	Kagooles Boys'	Orange	M L	2.90
D 612	Kagooles Boys'	Blue	M L	2.90
Socks				
L 976	Sportsocks	White/Blue Trim	8½–9½	0.75
L 977	Sportsocks	White/Red Trim	8½–9½	0.75
L 978	Over Knee	White	8½–9½	0.65
P 979	Socks Over Knee	White	10–11	0.70
L 980	Socks Double Thick	Grey Brown Fawn Black	Multi Fit	1.10

Index

Production Department (F85)   *11, 14, 91*
production system   *7*
program   *114*
programmable calculator   *80*
programmer   *114–16*
punched card   *26–9, 85*
  reader   *85*
  tape   *12*
Purchases Department (F85)   *11, 14*

quantative data   *2*
qualitative data   *2*

reports   *22*
RPG   *87*

Sales Department (F85)   *11, 14, 51, 174*
scientific
  calculator   *80*
  data processing   *76*
search key   *125*
security   *106, 108*
self checking numbers   *41*
services   *7*
silicon chip   *76*
software   *163*
  maintenance   *116*
sorter (card)   *27*
source document   *21*
stock requisition   *17*

systems
  analysis   *115*
  analyst   *116*
  design   *115*
  flowchart   *102*
  support   *104, 107, 114*

table   *130*
tally stick   *x, 19, 62, 74*
terminal   *101, 105*
test data   *116*
transaction file   *122*
transcription error   *39*
Transport Department (F85)   *11, 15, 24, 48, 121*
transposition error   *40*
transistor   *76*
trimmer   *112*

units   *2*
updating files   *122*
utility programs   *104*

verifier   *28*
verifying   *43*
visual display unit (VDU)   *99, 133*
voice
  output   *134*
  recognition   *134*

wages   *8*
word processing   *133*